Y0-BUO-525

Shenandoah Valley Folklife

Folklife in the South Series

Cajun Country
by Barry Jean Ancelet, Jay Edwards, and Glen Pitre

Kentucky Bluegrass Country
by R. Gerald Alvey

Upper Cumberland Country
by William Lynwood Montell

South Florida Folklife
by Tina Bucuvalas, Peggy Bulger, and Stetson Kennedy

Great Smoky Mountains Folklife
by Michael Ann Williams

Ozark Country
by W. K. McNeil

Carolina Piedmont Country
by John M. Coggeshall

Wiregrass Country
by Jerrilyn McGregory

Blue Ridge Folklife
by Ted Olson

William Lynwood Montell, General Editor, Folklife in the South Series

Shenandoah Valley Folklife

Scott Hamilton Suter

GR
108.2
.587
1999
west

UNIVERSITY PRESS OF MISSISSIPPI *Jackson*

For Holly

http://www.upress.state.ms.us

Copyright © 1999 by University Press of Mississippi
All rights reserved
Manufactured in the United States of America

02 01 00 99   4 3 2 1

The paper in this book meets the guidelines for permanence and durability of the Committee on Production Guidelines for Book Longevity of the Council on Library Resources.

Library of Congress Cataloging-in-Publication Data

Suter, Scott Hamilton.
    Shenandoah Valley folklife / Scott Hamilton Suter.
        p.   cm.—(Folklife in the South series)
    Includes bibliographical references and index.
    ISBN 1-57806-188-1 (alk. paper).—ISBN 1-57806-189-X (pbk. : alk. paper)
        1. Folklore—Shenandoah River Valley (Va. and W. Va.) 2. Oral tradition—Shenandoah River Valley (Va. and W. Va.) 3. Material culture—Shenandoah River Valley (Va. and W. Va.) 4. Shenandoah River Valley (Va. and W. Va.)—Social life and customs. I. Title. II. Series.
    GR108.2.S87 1999
    398'.09755'9—dc21   99-13966
                                                         CIP

British Library Cataloging-in-Publication Data available

CONTENTS

Folklife, a familiar concept in European scholarship for over a century, is the sum of a community's traditional forms of expression and behavior. It has claimed the attention of American folklorists since the 1950s. Each volume in the Folklife in the South Series focuses on the shared traditions that link people with their past and provide meaning and continuity for them in the present, and sets these traditions in the social contexts in which they flourish. Prepared by recognized scholars in various academic disciplines, these volumes are designed to be read separately. Each contains a vivid description of one region's traditional cultural elements—ethnic and mainstream, rural and urban—that, in concert with those of other recognizable southern regions, lend a unique interpretation to the complex social structure of the South.

Nestled between the Blue Ridge and Allegheny mountains, the Shenandoah Valley forms a natural corridor from south central Pennsylvania to the western parts of Virginia as well as Tennessee and North Carolina. As one of the nation's earliest western migration routes this fertile valley has seen successive waves of immigrants all of whom brought with them their own traditions and customs. *Shenandoah Valley Folklife* is the first comprehensive survey of this rich cultural heritage. Scott Hamilton Suter recounts the history of the valley's settlement, focusing on early Native American groups and the Germans, Swiss, Scots-Irish, and African Americans who eventually populated the region. He examines legends, musical traditions, traditional crafts, and long-standing religious groups, especially the Old Order Mennonites, the Church of the Brethren, and Baptists. Also included are discussions of architecture, foodways, fairs, and festivals that provide insight into how Shenandoah Valley residents have celebrated their diverse cultural traditions. Through a blending of historical research and contemporary fieldwork, Suter documents the region's traditional life, including the contributions made by recent immigrants who are adding their own traditions to long-standing customs, and demonstrates that folklife remains a resonant force in the Shenandoah Valley as it prepares to enter the twenty-first century.

The origins of this book lie somewhere in my past, since, growing up in the Shenandoah Valley, I spent my early days around many of the rural traditions that continue in the region today. My brother and I played in the large barns of Rockingham County and honed our baseball skills in its pastures. Not until I spent a semester studying traditional craftsmanship in Terry Zug's classroom in Chapel Hill, North Carolina, however, did I realize the significance of the regional culture in which I had the good fortune to grow up. Providence continued to smile on me; I next found myself under the tutelage of John Vlach. In his courses in the middle of urbane Washington, D.C., I learned to look at the traditions beyond the bucolic Shenandoah Valley and how to bring other experiences to bear on my native region. Many of the lessons these two taught me have found their way into this book, and I hope they will not mind taking some of the credit—or responsibility.

Much of the fieldwork reported here took place during the early 1990s, primarily as a part of a folklife survey of the valley that I completed for the Virginia Folklife Program, located at the Virginia Foundation for the Humanities and Public Policy in Charlottesville. I thank Garry Barrow for offering me the opportunity to participate in that project and for encouraging me to continue my work in documenting white oak basket makers throughout Virginia. His advice and encouragement have been welcome over the past eight years.

Other organizations have helped me along the way. The Shenandoah Valley Folklore Society generously provided a grant that enabled me to devote time solely to this project. The Harrisonburg-Rockingham Historical Society allowed me to use photographs from their impressive collection, as did the Winchester–Frederick County Historical Society.

I am also indebted to librarians and archivists throughout the Shenandoah Valley: Lois Bowman and Harold Huber at Eastern Mennonite University's Historical Library, Chris Bolgiano at James Madison University, Terry Barkley at Bridgewater College, and Nick Whitmer at the Rockingham Public Library all helped this project come together.

Throughout the writing of this book I have called on a number of people for advice and assistance; I received sound counsel whenever it was sought. My longtime friend and adviser, Cameron Nickels, commented specifically on the music chapter and, as he has on many other occasions, sharpened my focus on this project as a whole. Offering the perspective of a relatively recent arrival to the valley, Richard Gaughran's observations on its traditions often included thoughts that I, as a native, had overlooked. Richard also participated in the research on the Rockingham County Baseball League. John Stewart, whose own work appears throughout this text, graciously offered his insights into valley traditions and allowed me to use his vast fieldwork archives. It was an honor to work with him and to enjoy several lunches with him and his wife, Nancy. I am indebted to James Wilson, a historian of the region as well as a cultural geographer, for producing the map of the valley. Two former students gave me sound advice throughout this project: Richard D. F. Martin, a restorer of historic houses, provided insights into the material culture of the valley and served as a resource for books and articles not found on most bookshelves; Kevin Harter, another folklorist with a Chapel Hill connection, contributed his thoughts on music in the valley and read an early draft of the manuscript. His suggestions improved this book in many ways. Cheryl Lyon, a valley artist in many ways, offered suggestions on the text and lent her expertise to reproducing many of the images found throughout the book.

Throughout the years I have had the pleasure to play with many Shenandoah Valley musicians, and I am certain that numerous conversations with them regarding life in the valley have found their way into this work. I hope that all of these people will find some bit of their own thoughts here. I also thank the many informants who have taken the time to talk with me about their traditions for having the patience to endure my many questions. Without them this book would not have been possible.

Others have also contributed to the book in a variety of ways. Wayne Angleberger, Bill Cook, Glenn Cordell, Esther Dellinger, Janet and Earl Downs, the family of Byard and Nellie Early, David Edwards, Jeffrey and Beverley Evans, Maxine Layman, Dale MacCallister, the late Galen Miller Sr., Ernest Nicholas, the late Elmer Price Sr., Trish and John Rust, Elsie and Wilbur Terry, and Hubert Wine all helped make this book complete.

I learned a great deal about traditional life from my grandparents, Elizabeth and Ora Hamilton of Pendleton County, West Virginia, and Alice and Marion Suter of Rockingham County. I still consult with Grandma Suter on certain subjects. My parents, Norma and Stanley Suter, must be acknowledged for encouraging me to continue in this field of study as well as for offering their own opinions and memories about traditional life in the Shenandoah Valley and nearby West Virginia. And finally, I thank my wife, Holly, for enduring the writing of this work and for offering her own insights into folklife in the Shenandoah Valley. This book is dedicated to her.

The word *Shenandoah* has been used over and over for the names of towns, schools, mountains, caverns, and businesses and has even been given to a battleship of the U.S. armed forces. The name, however, is most often associated with Virginia's Shenandoah River Valley. Still, despite such a specific geographic location, there is debate about just what area is encompassed within the region known as the Shenandoah Valley. If you ask five residents of the valley where it begins and ends, you may receive five different answers. Through the years even scholars have disagreed on the answer to this question.

John W. Wayland, the most prolific historian of the region, offers the following concise definition: "The Shenandoah Valley, limited to the area drained by the Shenandoah River and its affluents, extends from the Potomac River at Shepherdstown and Harper's Ferry southwestward about 140 miles, nearly or quite near to the line between Augusta County and Rockbridge." Regional speech adds credence to this definition. Since the Shenandoah River flows due north, going "down the valley" is an acceptable way of saying one is going north, while going "up the valley" means one is heading south. Cultural geographer Robert D. Mitchell extends the valley farther south to the Natural Bridge, a prominent geological feature near the southern end of Rockbridge County. Parke Rouse Jr., chronicler of the Great Wagon Road that ran from Pennsylvania to Tennessee and Kentucky, is less precise in his definition, describing "the Great Appalachian Valley, whose northern end is called the Shenandoah and whose southwestern end becomes the Tennessee." With a romantic flare he adds, "The green Eden thus encompassed is called the Valley of Virginia."

Although the southern and northern boundaries of the Shenandoah Valley are the subject of debate, those to the east and west are not. The valley is bound by the Allegheny Mountains to the north and west and the Blue Ridge to the south and east. Beginning near Strasburg in Shenandoah County and running southwest approximately fifty-five miles, Massanutten Mountain bisects the central valley and separates the north and south forks of the Shenandoah River.

Following the river-based definition, the Shenandoah Valley includes the counties of Berkeley and Jefferson in West Virginia and Frederick, Clarke, Shenandoah, Warren, Page, Rockingham, and Augusta in Virginia.

Originally, all of these counties were a part of Virginia; however, when West Virginia was created during the Civil War, Berkeley and Jefferson Counties were included within the new state's boundaries because federal lawmakers wanted to maintain control of the main line of the Baltimore and Ohio Railroad, which ran through the area. Thus, political boundaries provided an artificial line where none existed geographically.

Historically, because of the role it played in the Civil War, Virginia has been seen as a southern state that exhibits all of the images of southernness found in the popular imagination—hillbillies, belles, and sharecroppers. While cultural ties to the South exist in much of the state, the Shenandoah Valley is certainly an exception, as this book will demonstrate. Many factors separate the valley culturally from the rest of Virginia, not the least of which is the Blue Ridge Mountains. The settlement patterns of the region led to an ethnic makeup that differed significantly from that of eastern Virginia, and this phenomenon contributed to a different culture in the valley. A study comparable to this one for the regions of Virginia east of the Blue Ridge would show the many different aspects of life throughout the state. This observation has long been apparent to Virginians; writing in 1895, valley resident Emanuel Suter wrote to his wife of a visit to his dying brother in Ohio: "The nurse rather confused his mind by telling him that I was his brother from Old Virginia. He understood that to mean what we call east of the ridge, he said he had no brother living there."

Although it is not necessary to belabor the point here, early residents of the Shenandoah Valley came predominantly from Pennsylvania, bringing with them many characteristics of that region rather than those of areas to the east settled primarily by the British. The study of the traditional life of the Shenandoah Valley reveals the close cultural ties with the territory north of Virginia and demonstrates the value of regional study within states. Eighteenth- and nineteenth-century valley residents clearly felt a cultural tie to the north, a feeling that many contemporary natives of the valley continue to experience today.

This book is divided into four sections that offer a glimpse at various aspects of traditional life, both historic and contemporary, in the Shenandoah Valley. Part 1 provides a brief history of the settlement of the region from the Native Americans to present-day immigration. This section provides the basis for an understanding of the discussions of folklife that follow. Part 2 explores oral and performance-oriented traditions in the valley. The Shenandoah Valley is well known for its contributions to both secular and spiritual musical traditions in the United States, and this section looks at historical and recent examples of such traditional music. Similarly, this portion documents the less well-known oral traditions of valley storytelling. Part 3 explores the variety of social institutions in the valley and affords an opportunity to examine religious expression as well as other traditional beliefs, including folk medicine and witchcraft. Also included here are discussions of cultural, historical, and ethnic festivals and fairs that celebrate traditional aspects of valley life. Part 4 deals with material aspects of valley culture, including historical and contemporary examples of folk art and craft. Providing further evidence of the importance of tradition in the lives of early and current residents, discussions of architecture and foodways round out the section. A conclusion ties these discussions together, creating a synthesis of the folklife of the Shenandoah Valley. An appendix contains a previously unpublished paper written in the 1960s by Elmer Smith and John Stewart, pioneers in the study of Shenandoah Valley folklife. The paper, an examination of the "evil weed" commonly known as masterwort, is indicative of the work they produced in the 1960s and serves as an example of both their pioneering work and their successful recording of traditions from elderly valley residents, many of them born in the nineteenth century.

Throughout this work I offer a range of examples, drawing on my own fieldwork and research as well as others'. Much of my work has been done through grants provided by the Virginia Folklife Program of the Virginia Foundation for the Humanities and Public Policy. As a result, this fieldwork reveals the limitations created by political boundaries—I have tended to explore only those valley counties located in the Commonwealth of Virginia. Still, I have used examples from West Virginia when available, and I believe that in many cases the illustrations chosen serve as general depictions of a particular tradition as it still exists in the Shenandoah Valley.

This book is intended as an introduction to the vast array of folklife in the Shenandoah Valley and draws on a wide variety of specific studies. I have tried to write for lay readers, pulling from the work of many others and condensing much information into one easily readable introduction. I hope that this book will provide readers with a new, more complete picture of life in the Shenandoah Valley and will inspire a new interest in the region's significant traditions.

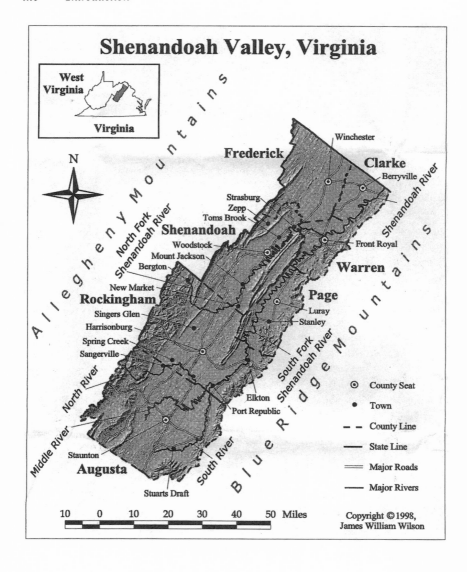

PART One

Settlement

When Virginia Governor Alexander Spotswood led his famous "Knights of the Golden Horseshoe" over the Blue Ridge Mountains in 1716, he claimed the beautiful land he encountered for England and was certain that he had found the paradise that Europeans had long sought in the lands to the west. Before Spotswood even, explorers such as Abraham Wood (1646) and John Lederer (1669–70) had reached the Appalachians but went no further. Gazing west over the hazy Shenandoah Valley from a pinnacle of the Blue Ridge, Lederer believed that he "had a beautiful prospect of the Atlantick Ocean washing the Virginia-shore." Despite the limited success of these early attempts to discover the secrets of the land to the west, by the 1730s the Shenandoah Valley was becoming a home to trappers and traders and quickly became a destination for settlers seeking fertile, unoccupied land. During the eighteenth and early nineteenth centuries, the Shenandoah Valley would become home to large numbers of Europeans, including Germans, Swiss, Scots-Irish, and English as well as smaller groups from other nations. The cultural traditions of these groups remain evident in the region today, and late-twentieth-century immigration to the valley has contributed new traditions to the centuries-old ones that have persisted through time.

People of the Shenandoah Valley

Natives

Although comparatively little is known about the Native American tribes that inhabited the Shenandoah Valley, archaeological finds over the past few decades have revealed more and more about the cultures of the people who lived in the region ten thousand years before the first Europeans built houses there. Evidence suggests that these early inhabitants would have encountered giant animals such as the woolly mammoth and the American mastodon—animals that they may have hunted, perhaps unsuccessfully. For example, one archaeological find revealed the bones of a mammoth that showed no signs of human butchering but included more than eighty projectile points. In 1891 a partial mastodon skeleton was discovered near the community of Singers Glen in Rockingham County, further testifying to the animal life encountered by the valley's earliest residents. While the mammoth and mastodon may have been more than a match for early hunters, the caribou that roamed the valley were probably more manageable and provided a ready source of food.

Evidence found along Flint Run and the south fork of the Shenandoah River suggest that innovations in the making and shaping of projectile points around 11,500 years ago enabled early valley residents to hunt more efficiently than was previously possible. In addition, the jasper in the area and easy access to the river made this area particularly attractive. Further evidence at this site demonstrates that the Clovis people may have resided there year-round. Furthermore, working at this site with his team of researchers, archaeologist William Gardner discovered a post-hole pattern that indicated an early dwelling consisting of a large, skin-covered dome structure—perhaps the earliest dwelling type in the valley.

As the Paleo period ended and the Archaic period began, the climate warmed and new species of plants and animals emerged, supporting a hunter-gatherer lifestyle. Natives hunted smaller animals such as elk and deer, and, although there was no agriculture, wild species of plants and animals allowed these residents to maintain a consistent culture. Berries, nuts, roots, and seeds contributed to the diet, and evidence suggests that food-grinding equipment such as mortars and pestles was used. In short, as the valley's environment changed, so did the lives of its early residents.

The material culture remains of these people are, of course, limited to those items that would not deteriorate over the centuries. Evidence of housing, fish weirs or dams in the Shenandoah River, projectile points, and other tools combined with ceremonial items such as beads and incised ornaments recovered from burial sites suggest that the people lived mostly in groups of twenty or thirty and that they moved seasonally within a limited territory. Other artifacts—antler headdresses, for example—indicate that a religious culture also existed. The ancient culture certainly would also have included games, chants, dances, and various rites of passage; however, these phenomena can only be conjectured.

Material culture provides the only indication of the change from the Archaic to the Woodland period, and archaeologists argue that the use of pottery is the major indication of a change in Native American culture in the valley. Data suggest that around 1200 B.C., clay pots were made of the area's abundant red clay and then dried in the sun. These early pots were built by hand, not turned on a wheel, but they proved very functional and indicate that a new, more settled culture had evolved. Archaeologists use different types of pots and their decorations to distinguish among centuries, but here it is sufficient to note that over time people became more and more settled, forming villages and developing agriculture to supplement their hunting-and-gathering lifestyle.

Author Darwin Lambert has compiled a cornucopia of the wild plants that native valley dwellers might have used, including gooseberries, crabapple, onions, moss, mulberries, wild peas, hog peanuts, persimmons, grapes, mushrooms, strawberries, and wild sweet potatoes. He also notes that along with the maple, the natives used several other trees to make sugar and syrup. Lambert's discussion concludes with his observation that the Woodland natives of the East used "an astonishing number of wild plant species—at least 130 for food, 275 for medicine, 31 in rites of magic, 27 for smoking, 25 for dyes, 18 in beverages or to flavor food, and 52 for other purposes."

Archaeologists speculate that despite this extensive use of plants, significant agricultural activity did not begin in the area until around 900 A.D., and even then crops accounted for only 25 percent of the diet. It appears that at least five varieties of corn were grown here and that all parts of the plant were put to use. Mats, rugs, or baskets, for example, could be made from the dried leaves. To accommodate their agricultural practices, the natives burned the land periodically, removing weeds and unwanted growth from cropland. New land for cultivation was cleared regularly, while old gardens were allowed to return to their natural states.

The primary source of food, however, remained animal meat, and deer and bear were the two most hunted and useful animals. Deer provided most of the Woodland native's meat and clothing, while the antlers afforded a variety of uses, including tools and projectile points. Bones and hoofs were also put to use. Bears offered some meat but primarily oils and hides, and claws were often used for ornamental purposes and sinews made useful bowstrings. Turkeys, too, were important for both their meat and their feathers, which were worn as ornaments or used on arrows.

Despite the thousands of years of their residence in the Shenandoah Valley, Native Americans left only a proportionally small record of their inhabitance. Perhaps their most significant and lasting contribution to the valley remains the name they gave to the region—*Shenandoah*. Similarly, the massive mountain range that knifes lengthwise down the valley also reflects the early native culture—*Massanutten. Allegheny, Opequon, Shawnee,* and *Tuscarora* are other Native American terms that remain as place-names in the valley.

Europeans

The European settlement of the valley was dominated by two groups—those of German and of Scots-Irish heritage—but representatives of other groups were also well represented in the region. While it was a natural route for those traveling to the western lands of America, the valley was itself a major destination from 1730 to the 1770s. During this period most of the valley's settlers arrived from southeastern Pennsylvania or came west across the mountains from the Tidewater area. By 1800 the total population of the valley had swelled to around eighty-four thousand, and others used the region as a temporary home on their way to Tennessee, Kentucky, and other areas of the South.

The Shenandoah Valley was not unknown to Europeans prior to 1730. Traders and fur trappers had been visiting the area since the seventeenth century, and, as noted earlier, it had been explored by Lederer and others in the 1670s. The native groups once common in the valley had not inhabited the region for some time before Europeans began to make forays into the area. Thus, settlement was made much easier and less violent than in other regions of the country. The valley did, however, remain a major route for Native American trading and war, and so early valley settlers did see periodic native traffic.

Although other land was available to those early migrants to the Shenandoah Valley, most notably in western Pennsylvania, there are many reasons why the valley became a destination. The natural accessibility from southeastern Pennsylvania seems an obvious motivation, as does the attractive, fertile land. Scholars have also noted that the uncertain Native American situation in western Pennsylvania detracted from movement in that direction, adding that colonial governments sought to use the Shenandoah Valley as a buffer zone between the British colonies on the East Coast and the French and their native allies in the West. All of these factors undoubtedly played some role in the decision to move into the valley, as Mitchell notes: "Although it would be inaccurate to attribute the significance of the Shenandoah Valley to any one major factor, the presence of a large area of broadly undulating, well-watered, fertile land, early perceived to be most suitable for agriculture and lacking permanent Indian settlements, could scarcely have failed to impress the earliest Europeans searching for favorable sites for settlement."

Landscape of the western Shenandoah Valley, 1998.

Perhaps the most obvious reason for the expanded settlement of the Shenandoah Valley was simply the extraordinary growth in Pennsylvania's population. Originally invited by William Penn in 1708 to settle in his colony, refugees from the besieged Palatinate region of Europe came in large numbers. By October 1709 nearly fourteen thousand had arrived in Pennsylvania. The groups of Swiss and Germans became so great that in 1717 the English governor, William Keith, requested that shipmasters carrying foreign passengers provide a list of their names. By 1773 nearly seventy thousand newcomers to the colony had been listed.

Around the same time, groups of Scots-Irish began to arrive. These people of Scottish ancestry were fleeing Ireland and the extremely high English taxes levied against them. Their added numbers in Pennsylvania contributed to population growth and led to English colonists' increased resentment of the rising flood of "foreigners."

Indeed, German, Swiss, and Scots-Irish ethnic traditions began to intrude on English customs, and such differences may have contributed to the movement of these groups out of Pennsylvania into Maryland and the Shenandoah Valley. Even-tempered Benjamin Franklin wrote in 1751, "Why should the Palatine boors be suffered to swarm into our settlement and, by herding together, establish their language and manners, to the exclusion of ours? Why should Pennsylvania, founded by the English, become a colony of aliens, who will shortly be so numerous as to Germanize us, instead of our Anglicifying them, and will never adopt our language or customs any more than they can acquire our complexion?"

Initially settling around Philadelphia, these groups eventually moved west and south in the colony, although they met with increased animosity from their English neighbors. Lord Baltimore, proprietor of the colony of Maryland, offered a liberal settlement package for these "newcomers" in 1732, thereby luring many settlers out of Pennsylvania. Baltimore's plan to bolster the population of his young colony worked, and Maryland's population swelled from 31,470 males above age fifteen in 1733 to 130,000 in 1756. Many of those moving out of Pennsylvania chose not to linger in Maryland, however, and by 1727 Germans began to appear in Virginia's Shenandoah Valley.

An exact date for the first German settlement in the Shenandoah Valley has never been determined; however, the first settlement for which there is documentation was started in 1727 by Adam Miller (Müller). Miller led his family and a few of his neighbors into the valley, where they settled along the south fork of the Shenandoah River between the Blue Ridge and Massanutten Mountain. Miller and his comrades had more than likely been sold on the valley by one of several Pennsylvanians who were touting the rich, open land of the Shenandoah. In fact, Miller recorded that his group had bought its farmland from Jacob Stover (Stauber).

Stover, Yost Hite, and John Van Meter are credited with being the first promoters of land in the Shenandoah Valley. They purchased tracts of land from the Virginia government and marketed it to groups of settlers hoping to find land outside of Pennsylvania, thus contributing significantly to the ethnic makeup of the Shenandoah Valley. Stover himself was the earliest resident of what is now Rockingham County. Hite moved to the valley in 1731, settling on tracts of a grant that Van Meter had procured. This land, located on Opequon Creek about five miles southwest of present-day Winchester, became a thriving community in the lower valley.

Following these early settlements along the eastern Massanutten range and Opequon Creek, the migration to western Virginia increased dramatically. This growing tide reached its peak in the mid-1740s, when much of the farmable bottom land had been claimed. Despite the lack of easily tillable land, however, many settlers—German, Swiss, and Scots-Irish— continued to come to the valley. Historian Klaus Wust suggests that the prospect of clearing land was no threat to most of these pioneers, since many had previous experience doing so. As Wust notes, "those who came to Virginia were the grown sons and daughters of the earlier immigrants, leaving their elders behind in Pennsylvania where German community life had already assumed certain normal patterns. Though many had been born in the old country, the young families represented a generation that had grown up in America."

During the first ten years of settlement, three distinct German areas developed in the valley, offering their inhabitants the comfort of community life. The first was the Massanutten colony, which stretched between the Blue Ridge to the east and Massanutten to the west, encompassing much of what is today Page County. The second was the Opequon group, which grew out of the original families living in the Hite area. The third, known as the Shenandoah colony, extended south from Strasburg along the western slope of the Massanutten. Eventually, as families grew and lands extended out of the immediate community, these three "neighborhoods" grew together to become one large German tract. There were also large groups of Scots-Irish in the area; in fact, much of the area of Rockingham County had a majority of Scots-Irish until the middle of the eighteenth century. Warren and Clarke Counties, however, were settled primarily by English settlers moving west from the Piedmont, and the number of Germans remained small in those areas.

After the Germans and Swiss, the Scots-Irish formed the next largest group to enter and settle in the valley. This group, called "Scots-Irish" because their ancestors were Scottish Presbyterians who had moved to Ireland in 1607 in response to favorable English offers to colonize that country, came to America for a variety of reasons. From the beginning of their settlement in Ireland, primarily in Ulster, the Scots built up a profitable linen and woolen trade. This industry eventually offered stiff competition to English manufactories, and in 1698 English wool producers convinced Parliament to suppress the Irish woolen trade. Along with this economic oppression, the Ulster Scots—as they are also known—faced religious persecution. Bishops of the Church of England who sat in Ireland's Parliament enacted laws that essentially required all officeholders to observe Church of England procedures. This requirement, of course, excluded all Presbyterians. Economic, religious, and political mistreatment led to the gradual exodus of the Scots-Irish from Ireland beginning about 1718. By 1740, when famine devastated Ulster, a major stream of immigrants began to cross the Atlantic Ocean for America.

Many of those who set out for America headed for Pennsylvania because of the colony's reputation for religious tolerance, naturally seeking out areas with existing Presbyterian communities, especially along the Delaware River. These established Ulstermen welcomed their compatriots, but, as mentioned earlier, the immigrants quickly wore out their welcome in Philadelphia and the surrounding areas and soon realized that they must venture west.

Just like enterprising land investors such as Hite, Stover, and Van Meter, wealthy eastern Virginia planters began to obtain grants for lands west of the Blue Ridge Mountains with an eye toward settling the region. Along with Lord Fairfax, William Beverley and Benjamin Borden Sr. obtained grants for large tracts of land in the 1730s and set about encouraging immigrants and emigrants to settle there. This land became a destination for the Scots-Irish moving out of Pennsylvania.

Beverley's grant of 118,491 acres of land in 1736 in what is now Augusta County was perhaps the most significant in shaping the settlement of the upper valley. Beverley Manor, as these lands came to be called, was intended solely as a moneymaking proposition for its proprietor. It is unknown to what extent Beverley advertised his lands; however, his intentions are clear from his 1737 letter to a ship's captain, James Patton, who often sailed to Ireland: "for we all propose to make money of the land & to that end I propose to hold it undivided & sell out & make ye most we can of it." Ultimately, few immigrants came from Ireland, but many came from Pennsylvania to buy this relatively cheap, unsettled land, which sold for pennies an acre and did not reach a shilling an acre until the 1760s.

Similarly, Borden acquired land solely for the purpose of settlement. A Quaker from New Jersey, he encouraged the Scots-Irish to move to his lands, which stretched south from Beverley Manor into current Rockbridge County. Borden received a grant of a thousand acres for every settler whom he persuaded to come to the valley, and his holdings eventually reached ninety-two thousand acres. As with the primarily German settlements in the lower valley, the upper valley was largely settled by Scots-Irish from Pennsylvania. Although pockets of other nationality groups did reside in the region, by the 1740s this portion of the Shenandoah Valley appeared on maps as the "Irish Tract."

These initial settlement patterns might suggest that cultural groups primarily stuck together and that the Shenandoah Valley became a region of culturally differentiated subregions. In terms of population, however, such was not the case. Mitchell writes that "territorial separation of national groups was rarely maintained over the long term. The residential mixing of ethnically diverse populations was the most dominant trend by the end of the colonial period." Cultural traditions were, however, often maintained, as the remainder of this book will illustrate. While areas of the valley were not the sole domain of specific ethnic groups, large proportions of one group or another did exist in these areas, introducing distinctive traditions that are still reflected in Shenandoah Valley culture.

Africans

Comparatively little is known about the growth of an African population in the eighteenth-century Shenandoah Valley. One of the earliest mentions dates from 1727, when a group of fifteen slaves escaped from a plantation in the valley near the headwaters of the James River, fleeing to near present-day Lexington. Evidence also suggests that Africans (voluntary settlers or slaves) were among the Germans, Swiss, Scots-Irish, and English who settled on Beverley's land grant in Augusta County. From the few resources available, however, it is clear that many more blacks resided in Berkeley and Frederick Counties during the eighteenth century. This fact is important, since, as Mitchell notes, "It was one of the most significant repercussions of Tidewater influences on the valley, and to some degree it created similarities in slave holding patterns between these two counties and the counties of the western Piedmont that were not to be found anywhere else west of the Blue Ridge."

With the help of tithing records, the distribution of Africans and African Americans in the late-eighteenth-century valley becomes more clear: a notable contrast exists within the region. By 1790, with 21.3 percent of its population listed as black, Frederick County was by far the leading slave-owning area. Frederick was followed by Berkeley County (14.9 percent), Augusta County, (14.4 percent), Rockingham County (10.4 percent), and

Shenandoah County (4.9 percent). As the valley developed into a region of its own, this discrepancy in the different numbers of slaveholders and nonslaveholders became a significant and divisive socioeconomic factor.

While many of the early slaves in the valley were undoubtedly brought there by Tidewater planters, it is also apparent that most slaves in the region were bought in Piedmont markets and brought over the mountains by farmers. Historian J. Susanne Simmons speculates that many of the Africans transported to the valley were children, lower in price because of their "outlandish ways" and thus destined to be sold to farmers on the frontier. This process, she continues, led to a deterioration of African cultural traditions as young Africans may have been placed in situations with American-born slaves who knew little of Africa and its culture and language.

The black population continued to grow in the valley, and, although most were slaves, some were free. The Virginia Assembly passed a law in 1793 requiring "free Negroes or Mulattoes" to register with the clerk of the court in the city or county where they resided. This registration took place yearly and demonstrates that there was a significant number of free blacks living in Virginia in general and in the Shenandoah Valley in particular. Registrations include whether blacks were emancipated or freeborn along with age and any distinguishing features. The listing of Polly McCoy of Rockingham County offers a representative example: "Registered in my office as No. 34 the 22nd October 1817 Polly McCoy (a free Woman of Colour) twenty five years of age the 6th day of March 1818 five feet Seven Inches high a Bright Mullattoe with dark Brown Eyes has three Moles on her face one at the left side of her mouth one between her Eyes and one below the right Eye she is the Daughter of Betty McCoy who was a free woman at the time of her Birth as appears by the certificate of William Parrott filed in my office." Such records now afford a priceless resource for learning more about this group of valley settlers, who are underrepresented in the scholarship of the region.

Recent Immigrants

More recent immigration to the Shenandoah Valley promises to bring new aspects of traditional life to the region. Beginning in the 1970s, Hispanic immigrants began to move into the valley to fill the large numbers of seasonal jobs offered by the apple industry. As the poultry business grew, many of these temporary residents stayed in the region, taking advantage of the economic opportunities presented by full-time employment. For many in this ethnic group, economic reasons are the sole reason for settling in the valley; immigrants, especially those from Mexico, often send much of their earnings back to family members in their native country. However, immigrants from El Salvador and Guatemala have come to the region as political refugees fleeing government persecution.

Using Rockingham County as a case study, it is clear that the number of immigrants is increasing yearly. U.S. Census figures for 1990 indicate that 1,315 Hispanics lived in the county at that time, a figure viewed as low by many observers. A 1997 survey conducted by the county's Refugee Resettlement Office suggests that a more realistic figure is 1,666, which, the office admits, is also a conservative estimate. Significantly, the Hispanic population has continued to grow, adding its own ethnic traditions to the array of centuries-old European traditions.

In the past decade, immigrants from Eastern and Central Europe as well as a small number of Southeast Asians have moved into the valley. With Russians and Ukrainians the largest group, these immigrants have come to the region for reasons similar to those of the eighteenth-century Germans, Swiss, and Irish: they are seeking relief from economic, political, and religious problems in their own nations. Often resettled with the help of religious organizations in the valley, those from the former Soviet Union came as religious refugees, abandoning their home countries, where only Russian Orthodox Church membership was allowed officially. Fleeing civil war and ethnic strife, Bosnians from the former Yugoslavia have also begun to resettle in the valley, particularly in Rockingham County. No U.S. Census figures exist for these groups; however, the Refugee Resettlement Office estimated in 1997 that their population numbered around nine hundred, making it a visible immigrant group in the county.

While extremely brief, this chapter serves as an introduction to the reasons for the settlement of the Shenandoah Valley and the groups of people who make the region their home. More importantly, this introduction sets the stage for a discussion of the valley's folklife. Traditions reflect the community that maintains them, and in the valley exist old traditions that directly link the region with the European nations that provided its earliest nonnative inhabitants. The remainder of this book will also demonstrate how traditions change, disappear, or are augmented by newly arriving groups with their own significant cultural backgrounds.

Folklife

Folklorists have long discussed the meaning of the words *folklore* and *folklife*, attempting to determine the value of one over the other. Basically, *folklore* refers to oral traditions as they relate to stories, songs, and beliefs,

Signs demonstrating the rural nature of much of the Shenandoah Valley, 1998.

while the term *folklife* encompasses all aspects of the everyday life of a regional, traditional culture. *Oral folk culture,* including those types mentioned above, refers to traditions that are primarily verbal and aural— ballads, for example. A community's traditional behavior is often referred to as *customary lore,* a phrase that incorporates religious activities, beliefs, and festivals of celebration. Unlike these two folklife genres, *material culture* refers to the traditional objects that a community produces. While the knowledge of how to make an item takes place in oral communication, the product of that knowledge receives the emphasis in material folk culture studies. White oak baskets, for instance, have long been crafted in the Shenandoah Valley, each one telling the story of its journey from tree to useful object. While separately they provide unique insights, taken together the branches of folklife offer a great deal to the overall understanding of a region's traditions.

PART Two

Performance

Unlike other aspects of traditional culture, oral traditions often require live performances to achieve their intended goal. Whether that intention is entertainment, spiritual inspiration, or the passing along of knowledge, the performances adhere to the community's accepted styles and methods. This statement holds as true for the Shenandoah Valley as it does for any region. This section looks at both secular and gospel traditional music, the Christmas traditions of belsnickeling, kriskringling, and shanghaiing, and oral storytelling traditions and demonstrates popular culture's role in determining the longevity and, in some cases, the vitality of folklife.

CHAPTER 2

String Music

Valley musician Cameron Nickels often humorously introduces an audience to his band's style of music by proclaiming, "The music we play is more eclectic than esoteric." Although intended as a joke, this statement aptly describes the string music that has become traditional in the Shenandoah Valley. While old forms of music continue to be played, popular music has also blended with the traditional, and this "new" music has become a part of the musical repertoire of valley folk musicians.

String bands, so called because they usually consisted entirely of stringed instruments, began to spring up in the valley in the late nineteenth century, although music was certainly played there before that time. In the valley, as elsewhere, the primary instruments included the fiddle, banjo, guitar, and cello, which eventually was replaced by the bass fiddle. In the time before recorded music, ensembles such as these played for dances and other formal or informal occasions. As Nickels's comment suggests, the music drew its inspiration from several sources. Traditional fiddle tunes certainly were prevalent, but classical and popular parlor music could also be heard at these functions. Similarly, music from immensely popular minstrel shows profoundly influenced the valley music scene. A playlist of turn-of-the-century Rockingham fiddler Ike Hudlow included such varied tunes as "Soldier's Joy," "Jenny Lind Polka," "Military Schottische," the waltz "Over the Waves," and Stephen Foster's "Darling Nellie Gray." At that time, valley residents were accustomed to hearing a wide variety of music and openly embraced this blend of traditional and popular tunes.

Fiddles were often the featured instrument, and it was not uncommon to find at least two in a musical group. Valley native Ellsworth Kyger, a fiddler himself, remembers his father's style of playing that instrument: "The Valley style was sedate. It followed a fairly good rhythm and a sensi-

Turn-of-the-century valley string band (*l. to r.:* Ben Long, Ike Hudlow, Will Long). (Courtesy Harrisonburg-Rockingham Historical Society)

ble pace." This was the common way of playing, and it tended to remain true to the way tunes were written. Kyger contrasts it with what he terms the "mountain style," which was faster and embellished with more notes. In the early 1900s, then, there was a clear distinction in the styles of local fiddlers, and valley musicians eventually drew from both sources, developing what has become a typical valley style in the late twentieth century.

While, like Kyger, many valley musicians learned to play from their family and community members, in the 1920s the influence of the radio began to show up in the musical selections that were heard in the region. Older musicians remember Saturday nights sitting before the radio anxiously waiting to hear the Grand Ole Opry on station WSM from Nashville. As A. O. Knicely recalls, "We'd have Grand Ole Opry music, popcorn, and sweet cider and so forth. That was a time, too, when some of the neighbors would come in. . . . Those were great times." Later, when he married in the 1930s, he and his wife, Frances, continued this tradition, listening to "the Grand Ole Opry on Saturday night and also WLW [Chicago] and

Wheeling, West Virginia. You almost looked to Saturday night because of this music." As musicians listened to the radio, broadcast programs began to change the tunes that people in the valley learned and performed. Now, more than seventy years later, these pieces have become traditional in the valley. Currently heard on only a few radio stations in the region, these old "popular" songs have become the traditional songs that have been passed along from generation to generation in the Shenandoah Valley. Tunes that originated on the minstrel stage in the nineteenth century are also played there regularly. "Arkansas Traveler" and "Turkey in the Straw," for example, are played from Frederick County up to Augusta, and most musicians learned them from interacting with others in the community, who may have in turn learned them long ago from an old-timer.

Along with the radio, television too has affected the traditional music scene in the Shenandoah Valley. Beginning in the late 1950s, Harrisonburg's WSVA offered the "Valley Barn Dance," a program hosted by the well-known bluegrass duo of Don Reno and Red Smiley. The program not only presented professional music to the area but also offered local musicians an opportunity to perform on television. Reno and Smiley and their guests brought the popular (at least in the South) sound of bluegrass into the homes of many who might not have otherwise heard it. Dalton Brill, a banjo player who learned to play from his father in the Shenandoah County village of Zepp, recalls, "I guess listening to Don Reno on channel 3 [WSVA] is where I probably picked up a lot of what I know." Prior to seeing Reno, Brill played a three-finger style but included double-string techniques and strumming—a sort of cross between the style popularized by Earl Scruggs and the earlier clawhammer method.

The Shenandoah Valley is certainly not unique in including popular music in the local traditional sound. There, however, it became the traditional sound. For example, children learned songs from the Grand Ole Opry in the 1920s and in turn taught their children, who then passed these musical memories along to their own young musicians. Accepted as part of the region's sound, these tunes have become a lasting part of its oral heritage.

Extending the life of music heard on the radio in the 1920s, A. O. and Frances Knicely's children and grandchildren have carried on their family's string-music tradition. In the 1970s the elder Knicelys formed a band with their children, traveling locally and playing bluegrass and gospel music. One son, Glen, continues to play bluegrass and country music regularly, and he and his wife, Darlena, have taught their three sons the pleasure of performing the music. All three can play a variety of instruments and one, now a member of a traveling bluegrass band, has also become a luthier, repairing as well as playing stringed instruments. Like many other

valley families that have passed along traditional music to younger generations, the Knicelys demonstrate the important role that music fulfills in
the family as well as in the community.

Today, bluegrass music is by far the most popular form of string music
in the valley. Bill Monroe is credited with developing the national musical
genre known as bluegrass by taking familiar mountain instruments and
tunes and blending them with parlor songs and ballads that many people
already recognized. The speed and ornamentation of the music—called by
one scholar "folk music in overdrive"—is akin to what Kyger identifies as
the mountain style of fiddling. Kyger points out that in the early days, "the
fiddlers on the radio were all going over to this, so eventually the mountain
style won out."

The popularity of this style is evident in the number of venues for bluegrass music in the valley. The region was in fact home to the first bluegrass
festivals in the United States. The very first, billed as the "world's biggest
bluegrass show," took place in August 1960 at Watermelon Park in Berryville, Clarke County. Featuring Monroe, Reno and Smiley, Mac Wiseman,
the Osborne brothers, and others, this event was definitely the most impressive gathering of bluegrass musicians to come together at that time. A
second festival, this one at Oak Leaf Park in Luray, Page County, was
staged in July 1961. Smaller festivals are still held throughout the valley,
attesting to music's importance to the community.

Gatherings at which local musicians jam with their neighbors are as significant as the festivals of professional musicians for perpetuating the
music in the region. Weekly sessions held at places like Raymond's Picking
Parlor in Mount Jackson, Shenandoah County, McCoy's restaurant in Stanley, Page County, or in the garage of Betty and Manley Allen's Stuart's
Draft home in Augusta County demonstrate area residents' strong ties to
this music. Similarly, impromptu sessions often arise at musicians' homes
as weekend social gatherings turn into evenings of music and visiting, often
surprising the uninitiated, who are unaware of the prolific traditional-
music scene in the region. In these places, musicians and nonmusicians
gather together to learn and enjoy the music. Raymond Bynaker, proprietor
of Raymond's Picking Parlor, sometimes finds the crowds that gather at
his place remarkable: "There are so many here playing [that] I have seen—
and this is honestly the fact—I have seen as much as four mandolin players
back here playing; four, five, six guitar players; three or four fiddle players;
as many as three basses on many a time; and as much as three dobros at a
time. . . . That's really too much, you know, but they're all enjoying themselves. And what of it? They're doin it for fun—nobody gets paid anything
for playing." Along with these unofficially organized sessions, performances sanctioned by grassroots organizations such as the Shenandoah Val-

ley Banjo and Fiddle Club and the Shenandoah Valley Folk Arts Revival Society help solidify the place of traditional music in valley life.

Old-time music, a style that adheres more to the fiddle and banjo styles of the mountains, is also prevalent in the valley. Learning "new" tunes from other devotees of this form of music, old-time musicians gather in each other's homes for sessions similar to those of bluegrass musicians. Often crowded affairs—old-time jam sessions can grow to as many as fifteen members—these get-togethers foster much improvisation and interchanging of tunes and techniques, inviting the oral tradition of the music to continue. In Rockingham County, for example, beginning in the 1970s area musicians knew that they could always find a weekend session at fiddler Edd Michael's barn near Port Republic, where they would meet other musicians, play music, and learn new tunes. Similarly, Wilbur "Two Gun" Terry, a well-known multi-instrumentalist, has hosted regular music parties at his house for more than twenty years. Such "happenings" encourage the vitality of traditional music by allowing young beginners to interact with seasoned veterans in an informal setting.

Although, like bluegrass, old-time music is popular worldwide, there remains an identifiable sound that is unique to the valley. The repertoire and tempo of the valley sound sets it apart from other regions of Virginia and neighboring West Virginia and North Carolina. Once, while playing with a group of unfamiliar instrumentalists in Richmond, Virginia, I was immediately identified as a valley musician because I "played hippy tunes," a term that remained undefined that evening but that clearly demonstrates regional differences and attitudes toward song selection and style. On numerous weekends, however, old-time musicians meet at conventions, events designed for acquaintances from throughout the region as well as other parts of the nation to renew friendships and learn and enjoy each other's music. At such events regional contrasts are noticeable, but these variations are often a source of humor and frequent admiration.

The valley is accepting of other musical traditions, and it is not surprising to hear Cajun and other ethnic music blended with the area's traditional sounds. Similarly, within the past ten years, the strains of Latino music have become more prevalent in the region, since the increase in the Hispanic population has naturally fostered the growth of this group's traditional entertainment. Dances at social halls and in local restaurants have encouraged not only those of Hispanic heritage but also others in the community to enjoy the sounds of *conjunto* and mariachi bands.

A folk ensemble consisting originally of a diatonic, button accordion, a Mexican guitar known as a *bajo sexto,* and *tambora de rancho* (ranch drum), the *conjunto,* or group, originated along the Texas-Mexico border in the 1860s. Commercialization led to the popularization of *conjunto* music in

Old-time jam session at Wilbur Terry's place, 1996. (Courtesy Kevin Harter)

that region in the 1920s, but the migration of Mexicans to other parts of the United States has brought the music to all regions where they settle. Originally associated strongly with the working class, *conjunto* continues, in the words of anthropologist Manuel Peña, "to articulate a Mexican working-class ethos. In its stylistic simplicity, its continuing adherence to the canción ranchera and working-class themes, and most importantly, in its actualization in weekend dances, the conjunto remains the bedrock music for millions of people whose everyday culture is Mexican at its core." An increasing number of social gatherings featuring this type of music demonstrates that Peña's observation holds true for the Shenandoah Valley, and the influence of *conjunto* on the region's traditional sound seems inevitable.

Ballads

While they were seldom accompanied by instruments, ballads have also remained a part of the traditional valley repertoire since the time of earliest

Advertisement for Hispanic bands in Rockingham County.

settlement. Similar to short stories set to music, ballads narrate brief dramas that consist of complication, climax, and resolution. The most studied of the genres of American folk song, ballads are often divided into categories that include medieval and broadside ballads. Ballads circulate widely throughout the United States, and, as in all traditions, variations occur in the lyrics, with the names of characters or places often changed to suit local tastes.

Founded in 1913, the Virginia Folk-Lore Society set about collecting ballads throughout the commonwealth, focusing only on those found in Francis James Child's collection of medieval ballads, *English and Scottish Popular Ballads,* better known as *Child Ballads;* in the Shenandoah Valley, ballad collectors recorded at least seventy-two ballads found in Child's volume. For a 1929 publication, Arthur Kyle Davis Jr. selected a representative sample from this collection and contributed an informative introduction to the ballad tradition in Virginia. His remarks quote one collector, Martha A. Davis, a teacher at Harrisonburg High School in Rockingham County, who wrote of her experiences in the valley in 1913: "The memory of the immortal ladies, 'The King's Daughter,' 'Barbara Allen,' and 'Lady Marget' [ballads found in Child's collection] is still fresh in western Rockingham. . . . This version of 'Barbara Allen' may be superfluous, but it seems worth while as a piece of genuine oral tradition. . . . [S]ome weeks ago I had the opportunity to hear the mountain woman sing again—the same [woman] who has given me quite a number of interesting ballads. This woman belongs to a clan that has lived in the hollow of the mountain near Swift Run Gap since pre-Revolutionary times, and there is not the slightest doubt that her ballads are genuine oral tradition."

The version of "Barbara Allen" to which Davis referred came from the mother of Wilmer P. Dove, who sang it to her son, who passed it along to Davis. The Doves lived, appropriately, in Dovesville (today the community of Bergton). What follows is Mrs. Dove's version of "Lady Marget."

> Sweet William he rose one May morning
>   And dressed himself in blue.
> "Come tell unto me that long, long love
>   That's betwixt Lydia Marget and you."

Unidentified nineteenth-century valley family. (Courtesy Harrisonburg-Rockingham Historical Society)

"I know nothing of Lydia Marget,
   Lydia Marget knows nothing of me;
But tomorrow morn by eight o'clock
   Lydia Marget my bride shall be.["]

Lydia Marget was sitting at her by-window,
   Combing back her golden hair;
And who did she spy but Willie and his bride
   At the churchyard as they passed by.

Down she threw her ivory comb,
   And back she threw her hair,
And down she fell from her by-window,
   Never to see there any more.

The day passed and the night came on
   When most men were asleep;
And who did appear but Lydia Marget's ghost
   A-standing at Willie's bed feet?

"Oh, how do you like your bed?" said she,
   And how do you like your sheep?
And how to you like that new married lady
   That is lying in your arms asleep?

"Very well, very well, do I like my bed,
   And better do I like my sheep;
But best of all is that young lady
   That is standing at my bed foot."

The night being gone, and the day came on,
   When most men were at work;
Sweet William said he was troubled in his mind
   Of a dream that he dreamed last night.

"Such a dream, such a dream, it can't be true,
   Such a dream, it can't be true;
I dreamed my room was full of white swine
   And my bride's bed a-lowing in tears."

He ask a leave of his many maids all,
   By one, by two, by three;
He ask a leave of his new married lady,
   Lydia Marget he might go to see.

He came and he knocked so loud,
   He called till he almost screamed;

And who was so early but Lydia Marget's brother
　　To arise and let him in.

"Oh, is she in the kitchen?" say he,
　　"Or is she in the hall?
Or is she in her highest chamber
　　Among her many maids all?"

"She's neither in the kitchen," says he,
　　"Nor is she in the hall;
She's lying under her cold coffin lid
　　With her pale face turned to the wall."

"Tears down, tears down those silk white robes,
　　Tears down those reannents so fine,
And let me kiss those clay-cold lips
　　That ofttimes have kissed mine.

"It was once I kissed her rosy cheeks,
　　It was twice I kissed her chin,
Three times I kissed her ruby lips,
　　But never will again."

Sweet William he died on eventide,
　　Lydia Marget she died on the morn;
Lydia Marget she died of pure, pure love,
　　And Sweet William he died from sorrow.

Ever in the churchyard green
　　Together they were laid,
And out of her grave grew a red rose,
　　And out of his a briar.
They wrapped themselves in a true lover's knot,
　　The red rose 'round the briar.

Reports such as Davis's demonstrate that even as late as the beginning of this century, oral traditions in balladry, particularly in the medieval genre, were maintained in the valley, although such a ballad tradition is no longer as evident as it once was.

Broadside ballads, so called because they were often initially printed on cheap paper and widely distributed in markets and by peddlers, also seem to have had a place in the Shenandoah Valley. These ballads often recount actual or fictional happenings in a sensational manner, chronicling events such as crimes, accidents, and relationships gone bad. A checklist of folk songs recorded in Virginia by the Federal Writers' Project between 1938 and 1942 reveals that a number of singers in the valley knew such ballads. The appearance of the titles "The Butcher Boy" (a tale of a broken heart and subsequent suicide) and "Charles Guiteau" (the story of the assassination of James A. Garfield) demonstrate that valley singers were rendering traditional songs of exciting and scandalous events as late as 1941. The following version of "The Butcher Boy" demonstrates the dramatic quality of broadside ballads.

In London city where I did dwell,
  A butcher's boy I loved so well,
He courted me my life away,
  And with me then he would not stay.

There is a strange house in this town,
  Where he goes up and sits right down,
He takes another girl on his knee,
  He tells to her things that he won't tell me.

I have to grieve, I'll tell you why,
  Because she has more gold than I,
Her gold will melt and silver fly,
  In time of need she'll be poor as I.

I went upstairs to go to bed,
  And nothing to my mother said,
Oh mother, she did seem to say,
  What is the trouble with my daughter dear?

Oh mother dear, you need not know,
  The pain and sorrow, grief that flows,
Give me a chair and sit me down,
  With pen and ink to write words down.

Go dig my grave both wide and deep.
  Place a marble stone at my head and feet,
Upon my breast, a snow white dove,
  To show the world that I died for love.

And when her father first came home,
  "Where is my daughter, where has she gone?"
He went upstairs and the door he broke,
  He found her hanging to a rope.

He took his knife and cut her down,
  And in her bosom these words he found,
A silly girl I am you know
  To hang myself for the butcher's boy.

> Must I go bound while he goes free?
>> Must I love a boy that don't love me?
> Alas, alas, will never be,
>> Till oranges grow on apple trees.

This ballad tradition continues today in the selections performed by many bluegrass singers, who recount in song narratives such as "The Wreck of the Old 97" (the saga of an unfortunate train wreck) and other ballads in the broadside style.

Gospel Music

Just as Scots-Irish pioneers brought the sound of fiddles to the valley, the choral sound of gospel music was perpetuated there by the Germans of all denominations who participated in congregational singing in their worship services. Church groups used hymnals that contained no music (the earliest were Pennsylvania reprints of European texts); however, since congregations frowned on the use of the instruments available at that time in worship services—fiddles, dulcimers, and flutes—there was often no musical accompaniment to the singing, and members relied on their memories for the tunes. Eventually Lutherans in Frederick and Shenandoah Counties acquired organs in the late eighteenth century, but most congregations did without such luxuries.

Despite this adherence to the choral singing of their ancestors, which led to a common belief that Germans were founders of singing schools in the valley, these immigrants were not in fact the originators of the movement toward teaching and popularizing choral singing. That honor lies with Ananias Davisson, a Presbyterian teacher who published a songbook in Harrisonburg in 1810. Called *Kentucky Harmony,* it introduced a new style of shape notes to the valley—reading of pitches following the fasola system, which featured unique shapes for different pitches. Part of a movement to simplify musical notation for those not familiar with standard notation, the term *fasola* referred to the last three syllables used in sight singing. The book was an immediate success among English-speaking congregations, a success that was not lost on the musical leaders of German-speaking groups.

This singing movement gained momentum in the South, leading to numerous publications, the most famous being *The Sacred Harp,* published by B. F. White and E. J. King in 1844, which gave its name to the popular shape-note system. This book, along with most others, taught the four-note fasola system; however, beginning in the 1840s a movement toward a seven-note system arose. Musicologist Kip Lornell points out that many young singers thought the new method progressive. The argument for the change was that there were seven different tones in the musical scales and therefore each should have its own name: mi, fa, sol, la ti, do, re. Eventually, many publications throughout the region featured the seven-note system.

While Davisson did initiate the singing movement in the region, Joseph Funk, a Mennonite schoolteacher, and several others must be credited with creating the works that today remain a part of the folk tradition of singing in the valley. Funk's first hymnal, *Die Allgemein Nutzliche Choral-Music (The Universally Useful Choral-Music Book)*, was published in Harrisonburg in 1816, but he is best known for his 1832 compilation first known as *Genuine Church Music* and later called *The Harmonia Sacra*, the title by which it is known today. Although only nine German chorales appeared in the book and all of the selections were translated into English, the work was extremely popular among Germans at the time: twenty-eight thousand copies had been printed by 1847.

The influence of Funk's work continued to grow following the Civil War, as his grandson, Aldine Kieffer, formed a publishing company with a friend, Ephraim Ruebush, in 1866. Over the next fifty years Ruebush and Kieffer's company worked diligently to popularize the seven-note system, publishing a series of songbooks along with a periodical called *The Musical Million*, a publication designed to encourage singing schools throughout the region. Kieffer also founded the South's first Normal Singing School at New Market in Shenandoah County in 1874, an event recognized as one of the most significant in the history of southern gospel music. Through the efforts of Ruebush and Kieffer, the seven-note system spread throughout the South as teachers using the company's publications scattered across the region.

Noting that by the late 1800s, singing conventions were being held throughout the South, Lornell points out that shape-note singing should be seen as a social form of religious music because it brings people together in groups for the sole purpose of singing. "Singings" from *The Harmonia Sacra* continue to be held annually in the valley, where large groups gather to continue the tradition of shape-note singing. Two traditional gatherings have a particularly long history. A sing has been held on New Year's Day at Weaver's Mennonite Church in Rockingham County since 1902. A similar gathering at the Mauck Meetinghouse—one of the oldest churches in the valley—in Hamburg in Page County also has a long history. These daylong events often draw hundreds of participants, who come to sing and bring food to enjoy at lunchtime. Ruth Furr, a participant at a 1967 Hamburg sing, commented on this aspect of the event: "Time to pause for lunch,

Participants from a *Harmonia Sacra* sing in Page County, 1940s. (Courtesy Harrisonburg-Rockingham Historical Society)

now, today, August, 20th century, and copies of *The New Harmonia Sacra* rest in solitude on the narrow benches. Outside, where through the trees, a feast beckons: fried chicken, meat loaf, salads, slaw, deviled eggs, pickles, cakes, puddings and pies, sour grape drink, and cold spearmint tea—you make choices with difficulty, while remnants of conversation blend with the sounds of summer."

As with the valley's secular music, participation in gospel music remains strong, and the traditions are maintained at gatherings where a new member of the group can be introduced to traditional ways of the past. Whether learning a new lick on the banjo or singing harmony from a 160-year-old hymnal, participants in traditional valley music maintain the standards created by the community over time. Although popular culture necessarily encroaches, valley musicians often re-create its sound, adding or subtracting to please themselves as well as those who listen.

Belsnickeling, Kriskringling and Shanghaiing

We'd put on great big old clothes, stuff 'em full of pillows and stuff, make ourselves look different than what we really looked, and put on false faces and go out in peoples' houses. Of course . . . you'd just go outside and holler and holler till they'd come to the door and invite you in. Just holler "Pelsnickels! Pelsnickels! Pelsnickels!" People knew it was somebody that knew 'em. Them days you didn't go anywhere unless you was a neighbor. They'd ask you to come in. And, back getting in my teens, we'd take the fiddle, mandolin, . . . and guitar, and 'course people knew about who we was without seeing us. You couldn't see us, but they knew about who we was. We just had the biggest times.

                                        Lester Ryman, Shenandoah County

Many people in the Shenandoah Valley experienced Lester Ryman's "big time" during the Christmas and New Year's season. Ryman describes an evening of belsnickeling (or pelsnickeling, as Shenandoah County residents call it), a tradition widespread in the Shenandoah Valley up to the early 1960s, when it died out. This custom was a large part of some valley residents' Christmas celebrations for years, and it represents a significant traditional activity.

Belsnickeling, and its close relatives kriskringling and shanghaiing, originated in Europe. Folklorist John Stewart notes that the words *belsnickel* and *kriskringle* are derived from German: "*Belsnickel* contains the word *Pelz* (fur) as well as St. Nicholaus (Santa Claus). *Kriskringling* is a derivative of *Christkindel* or Christ child. Santa Claus, *Belsnickel* and *Krisk-*

Lester Ryman.

ringle are thus essentially the forerunners of our present-day Christmas customs."

Like many valley traditions, these three derived from Pennsylvania German customs. Two nineteenth-century writers attest to the existence of the belsnickeling tradition in Pennsylvania, one recalling that "all Pennsylvania German children look forward to [Christmas Eve] with great anxiety. That is the evening for the 'Belsnickel' to put in his appearance in hideous disguise to look after naughty boys and girls, and he distributes his gifts in the shape of nuts and cakes, throwing them on the floor; woe to any youngster who dares to pick up any of them—he will be sure to get a sound whack on his back with a whip." In the Shenandoah Valley, belsnickelers were not such feared characters but instead welcomed revelers, and the time for visiting was extended from the week before Christmas until New Year's Day.

Valley belsnickeling essentially consisted of dressing up in costumes made of old clothes, gloves, and masks, either homemade or store-bought, and then visiting neighbors. The belsnickels would talk with the home owners, who would attempt to guess the bizarre visitors' identities and serve some sort of refreshment. Dalton Brill offers the following description of what happened once belsnickels were invited inside: "You'd go in, and you'd mingle around with the people and talk to the people and have 'em to try to guess who was who. So if they'd guess you, then if you had a false face on, you'd take the false face off. And if they didn't guess you, you'd leave it on. And if they didn't guess you, well, then they'd always give you a treat of candy, cake, maybe a little moonshine, and drinks of that sort, and then you'd kind of visit with them, and then everybody would take their faces off and visit, and go to the next house." Music often played a role, and both Brill and Ryman recall taking their instruments along.

Both young and old participated in this custom, although, as one informant recalled, alcohol was occasionally a part of the evening's fun, and sometimes only those deemed old enough to drink liquor took part.

> It was more older people. . . . I know one time that I took my father and my uncle and about five or six other older guys—my cousin and I did. We decided to get them all together and take them pelsin' 'cause they used to really like to do it. Of course, we took some whiskey along. We kept feedin' 'em the whiskey. And, of course, they knew everybody in the community, so they all dressed up—my daddy and my uncle—and [put] false faces on, and beards and all. They'd changed themselves. And they was good at fooling people,

Unidentified belsnickels in Singers Glen, Rockingham County, c. 1910. (Courtesy Harrisonburg-Rockingham Historical Society)

they really could. So about the last place we went to, they was all gettin' just real high, so they said "we're going to have to stop at Mr. Spicher's house, we want to pelse him." So we pull up in his driveway, my daddy and my uncle they go up and knock on the door and holler, "Would you like to see a pelse?" Well, Spicher, he opened up the door, "Yeah, come on in Raymond, Herbert, yeah come on in." They'd forgot to put their face on! Oh, they got mad about that!

Despite the occasional presence of spirits, however, teenagers often belsnickeled in their communities. Remembering the 1930s, one woman noted that she frequently tried to fool her own parents, sometimes with success.

In their fieldwork in the valley in the early 1960s, Elmer Smith and John Stewart found that the custom of kriskringling was observed only in eastern Rockingham County, although the same term has been used in Grant County in eastern West Virginia. The custom was essentially the same as belsnickeling. Smith and Stewart's informants told of nighttime excursions dressed in costumes, but the pair found that those areas had fewer residents of Pennsylvania German heritage, suggesting one explanation for the difference in terminology.

It should also be noted that not all valley residents of German heritage participated in these merriments. Members of the conservative Mennonite and Brethren religious groups frowned on what they viewed as unchristian behavior. The minute book of the Cooks Creek Church of the Brethren records that in February 1883, "Daniel S. and Letcher Karacofe were charged with disguising themselves with Masks and otherwise in an unbecoming manner—and joined in with others of similar array in procession through the neighborhood and John Michael Flory was charged with encouraging this unchristian conduct by inviting said parties to his house—for which the church demand a satisfactory confession on or before the next council meeting." Two of these transgressors were "disfellowshipped" (excommunicated from the Church) for not appearing to make the required confessions. To conservative groups such as these, such traditional activities amounted to making a mockery of the Christmas holiday.

Shanghaiing, the third of these Christmas customs, has obvious similarities to the other two; however, there are significant differences as well. As in belsnickeling and kriskringling, the participants dressed in outlandish costumes and went about their neighborhoods. Shanghaiing, however, took place during the daytime and involved parading through the streets on horses or mules or in wagons and sleighs. An informant from Augusta County described shanghaiing in detail: "In the 1890s, groups went shanghaiing near Staunton. They rode horses in groups of six or eight. They were always masked and dressed in costumes. They went about in daylight hours and stopped at a home occasionally, making noise and blowing horns, but they did not come in. They also went shanghaiing in the Spring Creek, Moscow, and Spring Hill communities [located near the Augusta–Rockingham County line]." Horses were often decorated as well, and it seems clear that the whole idea was to have fun. Noisemakers and horns always attracted attention, and occasionally liquor was added to the mix.

In 1960, a Spring Creek resident enthusiastically recalled shanghaiing near his home:

> Shanghai! That there used to be quite a time through this country. They would gather up here from all over the country. I've seen 'em go down the road here and have a string of 'em sometimes nearly a mile long. Dressed in all kinds of uniforms and costumes, riding mules and horses, some of 'em would be in buggies, some in spring wagons, and some would be horseback, maybe two or three on an old mule. They'd nearly always have one would come along behind, he'd be a good little ways behind, a couple of 'em, riding an old mule, this old mule he'd be a little balky every now and then. . . . Come to a mud hole, he'd stop. Maybe they'd get spilt off before they got through a mud hole. He wouldn't want to cross a creek or something, he was just sort of kind of bringing up the rear. But they was just out for a jolly good time. . . . Never heard of 'em causing any trouble or bothering anybody or molesting anything; they just going through the country. They'd usually start early in

Shanghais, c. 1910. (Courtesy Dale MacAllister)

the morning, wouldn't be back 'til that night sometime. . . . I reckon the last time I ever saw anything like that was along about 1914 or '15.

This colorful recollection suggests the high level of community involvement in this yearly custom.

While belsnickeling and kriskringling seem to have identifiable antecedents in Pennsylvania and Germany, shanghaiing's origins remain a mystery. A few of Smith's and Stewart's informants knew all three terms but used them interchangeably, and there is no precedent for shanghaiing in Pennsylvania. The custom seems to have been relatively unknown except among a group with German ancestry living in the valley in an area (Augusta County) that borders a predominantly Scots-Irish area, suggesting that the tradition may have originated among the Scots-Irish.

Stewart has postulated several origins for this tradition of shanghaiing: the most plausible draws a parallel to the Celtic celebration Samhain. This day was originally the Celtic celebration of New Year's and was celebrated on 1 November. It was also a day of the dead on which spirits were believed to be wandering about on the earth. The festivities of the day included lighting bonfires and preparing special foods. Significantly, it was also a custom to dress as and mimic spirits. Animals, too, were costumed. Eventually Christianized, the day became All Saints Day, but it is significant to note that on that holiday's eve (Halloween), people still dress in costume and proceed through their neighborhoods. A final possibility for the activity's name may come from within the agricultural community. Introduced to the United States about 1845, the Shanghai chicken was a large bird with unusually thick, fluffy, and often elaborate plumage. Perhaps to "go shanghaiing" meant to dress in colorful and unusual costumes and strut through the neighborhood.

Regardless of the origins of such traditions, they no longer take place in the valley. When Smith and Stewart were doing their fieldwork in the early 1960s, there remained a strong feeling of community in villages, and residents recalled visiting socially on a regular basis. Informants in the 1990s, however, told me that during World War II people began to be suspicious of others, and this feeling led to a fear of wearing masks in public. Ryman suggests that "people were getting more cautious, . . . more dubious of letting people into their houses." Ultimately, an influx of residents from outside the community—displacing accepted customs and beliefs, as well as the sense of security—may have contributed as much as anything else to the demise of these Christmas traditions.

Folk Narratives

Folklorists use the term *folk narrative* to describe traditional stories that are told directly to an audience. These stories have many forms but most often fall into the broad categories of myth, legend, and tale. Dan Ben-Amos has summed up succinctly the differences among these three types of oral narrative, suggesting that they "are taken to differ from one another in their relation to cultural conceptions of truth and reality. Myth (from Greek *mythos*) is believed to be true, legend (from Latin *legenda*) purports to be true, and folktale is inherently untrue—only fiction and fantasy." These types exist in many cultures; however, in the Shenandoah Valley, as in most regions of the United States, increased literacy and modern advances in communication have dramatically cut down on the traditional ways of passing along information and entertaining through storytelling.

Although there must have been many traditional narratives told early in the valley's history, including Native American myths, a collection of Shenandoah Valley folk narratives has never been compiled. Numerous local historians have added a variety of legends to their works over the years, and John L. Heatwole has recently collected anecdotes about valley residents and happenings, but no systematic collection has been undertaken.

As early as 1833, Samuel Kercheval, the first historian of the valley, lamented that the once ubiquitous Jack tales carried over the Atlantic from Europe had disappeared from the mouths of valley residents. These tales, typically involving a protagonist named Jack who acquires a magical object or extraordinary power, demonstrate the self-reliant qualities valued on the frontier: perpetually an underdog, Jack always triumphs over adversity. Kercheval described the tales that he remembered as a young man: "Dramatic narrations, chiefly concerning Jack and the Giant, furnished our young people with another source of amusement during their leisure hours. Many of those tales were lengthy, and embraced a considerable range of incident. Jack, always the hero of the story, after encountering many difficulties and performing many great achievements, came off conqueror of the Giant. Many of these stories were tales of knight-errantry, in which case some captive virgin was released from captivity and restored to her lover." Noting the educational as well as the entertaining quality of these tales, Kercheval traces their origins back to Homer's time, suggesting that they "certainly have been handed down from generation to generation from time immemorial." But valley residents no longer told such tales of valor, according to the author. Noticeably perturbed, he wrote, "Civilization has indeed banished the use of these ancient tales of romantic heroism; but what then? It has substituted in their place the novel and romance."

Television, film, and video games have now replaced the oral narratives of heroism and romance; however, traditional narratives are still told in the Shenandoah Valley. Most often they take the form of legends—stories that tellers usually believe to be true but whose veracity listeners must judge for themselves. Many of these stories concern supernatural events and ghosts that haunt a neighborhood house or piece of road. One of the most famous of Shenandoah Valley legends regards the strange occurrences that took place early in the nineteenth century on the Augusta County farm of Dr. John McChesney. The following version of the events is taken from Joseph A. Waddell's *Annals of Augusta County*, first published in 1901.

William Steele [Dr. McChesney's nephew] is now (1889) one of the few surviving witnesses of the occurrences to be related, and to him we are indebted for all our detailed statements. He was a child at the time, six years of age, but distinctly remembers what he saw and heard; and, we may add, his veracity is unquestionable. His testimony before any tribunal in Augusta county would be implicitly believed.

In 1825, Dr. McChesney's family consisted of his wife, four young children, and sundry negro servants, one of the latter a girl named Maria, probably eight years of age. One evening in January or February, while the white family were at supper, Maria came in from the kitchen, which was 20 or 30 feet from the dwelling, very much frightened apparently, and saying that an old woman with her head tied up had chased her. Little or no attention, however, was given to this incident. But Maria continued for some days to complain of being frightened when by herself, and other circumstances connected with the girl attracted the attention of the family. Soon after this, vollies of stones began to descend upon the roof of the dwelling house, and continued to fall at intervals, in day-time and also at night. The stones averaged about the size of a man's fist, and some of them were too large to be thrown by a person of ordinary strength. Occasionally, some of the stones were hot, and scorched the dry grass on which they fell.

Reports of the stone-throwing circulated through the country, and hundreds of people from miles around came to witness the spectacle. On some days the yard was full of people, on all sides of the house, eagerly watching to see where the stones came from; but all retired without making any discovery. The descent of stones did not occur every day, and visitors on the off-days generally went away incredulous about the whole matter. During the whole time Maria complained of being chased and frightened.

As Maria seemed to be the centre of the disturbance, Dr. McChesney concluded to send her away, and ordered her to go to the residence of his brother-in-law, Mr. Thomas Steele. While she was on the way across the hills, Mrs. Steele and her children (including her son William), a young white woman, and a negro woman and her children were under a tree in the yard. Mrs. Steele was knitting, and the negro woman was engaged in washing. Mr. Steele was not at home. Suddenly a loud noise was heard in the house, as if it were full of frightened and stamping horses. The white woman ran first to the house, and called Mrs. Steele to come. In the centre of the large room all the movable furniture was piled up promiscuously,—bed, bureau, chairs, andirons etc. While the spectators were looking on and wondering, stones began to fall on the house, and then Maria was seen approaching. She stated, as usual that she had been chased by an old woman, and her evident terror was distressing to behold.

Maria was sent home, but the fall of stones continued at Mr. Steele's. The missiles entered the house, how and from whence no one could discover, and broke the glass in the cupboard doors and many of the plates and dishes. The furniture was severely pelted, and some articles still preserved show the marks to this day.

There was no cessation of the occurrences at Dr. McChesney's. One day in the spring, the weather was still cool, the family were sitting around the fire. The persons were Dr. and Mrs. McChesney, Mrs. Mary Steele, Mr. and Mrs. Thomas Steele, their son, William, and others. The doors were closed and the window sashes were down, when a stone, seeming to come from a corner of the room, near the ceiling, struck Mrs. Thomas Steele on the head. She was the only person struck at any time. A lock of her hair was severed as if by scissors, and her scalp was cut to the bone, causing profuse bleeding. Mr. Steele became enraged, and denounced the invisible agent for "taking its spite on a woman," and not on him. He then took his seat in the front door, and immediately was pelted with clods of sod and earth, coming from the inside of the house. He sat there till the missiles were piled around him, and then, at the earnest solicitation of his mother, who cried that "the thing" should kill him, left the spot and was not pursued.

Wishing to remove the McChesney and Steele children out of the way, they were sent to their grand-mother's near Midway; but Maria was sent also. Soon the disturbances began at Mrs. Steele's,—stones flew about, furniture in the kitchen moved of its own accord, etc., etc. One day a large kitchen bench pranced over the floor like a horse. The children present were at first amused, and young John M. Steele proposed to bridle the steed and ride him. They did so, but became so much alarmed at the antics of the bench that young Steele fainted. During this time, Mrs. Steele's farm servants found that food and tools taken by them to the fields, disappeared and turned up at the house.

While at Mrs. Steele's, Maria frequently complained of being beaten. Mrs. Steele took her between her knees, drew her skirt about her, and with a stick struck around as if to beat off an invisible foe. Maria continued to cry out that she was beaten and pricked with pins. The "slaps," says William Steele, were distinctly heard, but no one could see the vindictive enemy. At last the victim fell upon the floor, exhausted and apparently dead, but soon revived. She continued to be punished as described for many weeks.

Worn out with these troubles, Dr. McChesney, as a last resort, sold Maria, and she was taken South. As soon as she left the disturbances ceased and they never followed her in her new home.

An old negro woman lived in Dr. McChesney's neighborhood, who was reputed to be a witch. William Steele says "she walked with a stick and chewed tobacco," and that in his boyhood he was always careful to give her the road when they met. It was said that this old woman received some impudence from Maria, who had an evil tongue, and threatened her with punishment. Of course, readers who believe in witches understand now why and from whom the troubles came! We have no explanation or theory to advance. We cannot, however, refuse to believe that many strange things happened, as related, without repudiating all human testimony.

Similar occurrences have taken place in Rockingham, Albemarle and Culpeper counties, the last in 1889.

Although Waddell could only report what had occurred up to the time of his writing, recent owners of the McChesney house and farm report that strange events continue to happen there. Within the past twenty years livestock have been moved into different fields overnight; fence gates have been turned upside down, doors have mysteriously become locked, and objects have moved unexplainably within the house. As with any legend, listeners/reader must judge for themselves.

At the other end of the valley, in Frederick County, ghosts have also been known to appear. The following narrative, here in the words of John

L. Heatwole, further demonstrates the question of "believability" of legends.

> Out on the old Northwestern Pike, west of Winchester in Frederick County, there was a two-story house where [a] peddler was rumored to have been murdered. Once, when a couple of children were in the residence, he made himself known to them.
>
> In one lower room there was an enclosed staircase with a door. The brother and sister often played in this particular room. They had heard the stories the adults told about the ghost, and they wanted to believe. One time, when they were playing with cut-out paper animals on a table in the room, the latch to the staircase door raised up and down, over and over again. The sound of clicking metal aggravated the boy, and he called out, "Come down, if your nose is clean!" Soon it was discovered that no one was on the staircase or in the room above.
>
> The peddler's ghost appeared one night. The girl awakened in her room and saw a man with a long, grey beard leaning over her bed and staring at her intently. Hastily brushing the sleep from her eyes with the backs of her hands, she looked again, wide-eyed, and he was still there. She let out a gasp and threw the covers over her head, and when she got up nerve enough to look again, he had disappeared.
>
> In the light of day, the little girl thought that the apparition must have been a dream, after all, but when she told her brother about it he related that he, too, had been visited by the old, grey-bearded man.

This legend offers a good example of what folklorists refer to as *motifs*, or striking narrative elements. A motif may be an object, an action, a character or any of a number of elements that have been organized in *The Motif Index of Folk-Literature*, the work of folklorist Stith Thompson. This reference tool is a collection of thousands of motifs, each categorized with others that are similar. As with most regional legends, motifs found in the above story appear in other legends from other parts of the country and around the world. This legend, for example, demonstrates Thompson's motif E 421.5: "Ghost seen by two or more persons; they corroborate the appearance."

Another legend concerning the McChesney place offers a good example of motifs and how they can be compared in different stories. Heatwole recounts how a man "had been sitting peacefully by his hearth when all of a sudden the tongs left their place and started to dance about, mystifying the observer. He got to his feet, grabbed the tongs and put them back in their normal spot as he yelled, 'Get back there, damn you!' They immediately jumped out again and danced around the room. The man grabbed them a second time, but there was a struggle and magically the tongs burned the man on his left leg." Despite the lack of specificity regarding the details when compared to the previous McChesney legend, this one does offer an interesting comparison when the motifs are examined. Recalling the episode of the kitchen bench prancing about the room, the account of the fireplace tongs takes on significance beyond that of an interesting legend. Both stories, while different in details, include Thompson's motif E 599.6: "Ghosts move furniture." Folklorists are interested in the recurrence of motifs and where they appear. The fact that the same motif appears in two different legends about the same place, as occurs in this case, raises questions about regional beliefs and storytelling techniques.

Another type of legend, perhaps the most common in the Shenandoah Valley, is the anecdote, or short personal legend. These stories about a local character are usually false but are told as if they were true. Most towns and villages have had individuals whose personalities lend themselves to these types of apocryphal stories. These legends may contain elements of the supernatural, but most often they reflect something about the individual in question, as in this narrative recorded by Heatwole.

> Early in the 20th century, near the lovely village of Singers Glen in Rockingham County, there lived a very mean old man. How mean was he? He was so mean that his favorite pastime was to sit on his front porch and shoot every bird that alighted on the fence that separated his yard from the road. He didn't care if the bird was a crow or a cardinal, a bluejay or a dove—he shot them all. For years he killed every bird that was unfortunate enough to select that particular fence to rest upon.
>
> Well, eventually the old man came to his own end. His body was removed from the house and prepared for burial, and on the day of the funeral, following the church service, his casket was carried down the road toward the cemetery. As the procession approached the dead man's house, everyone plainly saw that his fence, so long an execution site, was lined thickly with birds bearing witness to a terrible enemy's passing.

Other local anecdotes are more humorous and often deal with the strength or superior prowess of an individual. For seventy-five years the valley has been the home of the Rockingham County Baseball League, one of the nation's oldest continuously operating amateur leagues. This long history has naturally spawned some legendary heroes. The late Galen Miller Sr., the last living player from the inaugural season of 1924, remembered many stories from the league's past. In 1995 Miller, a lifelong resident of the village of Spring Creek, recalled a game from around 1930 that drew an estimated crowd of two thousand—the hamlet's largest ever—as the Spring Creek nine hosted the rival Bridgewater team. In a truly legendary account, Miller recalled that Bridgewater had "the bases loaded and

Rockingham County Baseball League action in Spring Creek, c. 1950. (Courtesy Hubert Wine)

Gilbert Long [a famed home-run hitter] come up to bat and the [pitcher] threw 'em a way away from him. [Long] jumped clean up in the air and hit the ball and knocked it over the fence—but it was foul. And from then on [the pitcher] rolled 'em in there. When [Long] come to bat, he just rolled the balls in. [Long] couldn't hit 'em. Now that's fact." Bridgewater won the game, twenty to seventeen, but the story of Long's intentional walks on balls rolled along the ground overshadows the score.

Legends such as these continue to make their rounds in communities throughout the Shenandoah Valley. Seldom believed as official history, they record fantastic, amusing, and instructive happenings, keeping a regional flavor while using many of the same ideas as stories from other areas. Folklorists have long known that myths, legends, and tales from around the world bear similar motifs and story lines, and many of those found in the valley's narratives also appear throughout the world. Along with these similarities, the localities, individuals, and stories themselves add to the regional flavor of the narratives, making each uniquely "valley" in its content.

PART Three

Social Institutions

In certain respects, this entire book concerns social institutions, since it deals with a variety of communal systems and beliefs. In this section, however, the term refers to institutions and ideas that draw people together, especially their religion and beliefs, their work, and their ethnicity. In some cases these categories overlap, and yet they often differ from group to group. For example, there are many religious organizations in the Shenandoah Valley, each with its particular traditions and beliefs. Often, however, beliefs about why things happen or how to control aspects of life are more traditional than officially sanctioned.

Gatherings of like-minded groups form an integral part of the valley's past and present. Whether religiously, occupationally, or ethnically oriented, these assemblies tell a great deal about traditional life in the Shenandoah Valley. By taking a look at representative religious groups in the region as well as at a variety of festivals, this section will offer insights into how social organizations have encouraged the maintenance of tradition as well as promoted regional culture.

CHAPTER 5

Folk Religion

A well-known folklore textbook states that "religious folklore is folklore that has to do with religion." The simplicity of this remark is deceiving, however. How do we find traditions within institutionalized religions, and what, if anything, separates the mythology of written holy texts from the traditional beliefs of the people who make up a particular religious group? These are difficult questions with which many scholars have struggled, and entire books have not answered them successfully. Here, I simply present traditional aspects of three religious groups—Baptists, Mennonites, and Brethren—that are historically associated with the Shenandoah Valley, offering a comparative look that provides insight into both the past and present in the valley.

While the terms *folk religion* and *religious folklore* seem quite similar, their meanings differ, and this chapter focuses on the former. The term *folk religion* has been defined in various ways over the years; however, folklorist Don Yoder's definition is perhaps the most concise: "Folk religion is the totality of all those views and practices of religion that exist among the people apart from and alongside the strictly theological and liturgical forms of the official religion." Essentially, religious groups that follow strict, written rules in their worship services differ from those that rely more on beliefs and a less formal structure.

Offering another perspective, William Clements suggests, "Folk religion differs from official religion only in its lack of association with the society's power structure." Clements also lists ten traits that he feels often exist in American folk Protestant churches:

1. Scriptural literalism
2. Orientation toward the past

3. Consciousness of God's providence in human affairs
4. Emphasis on evangelism
5. Informality
6. Emotionalism
7. Moral rigor
8. Sectarianism
9. Egalitarianism
10. Relative isolation of the church building (away from political, social, and economic centers).

Clements is quick to point out that these are generalizations and that different groups have varying degrees of these traits: some have all; some have none. These traits do, however, provide a useful basis to keep in mind while looking at folk religion in the Shenandoah Valley.

The Fellowship Independent Baptist Church

In a series of studies of folk religion in the Valley, folklorist and ethnomusicologist Jeff Todd Titon explores the importance of tradition in the lives of members of one Baptist church in Page County, the Fellowship Independent Baptist Church. In his work, which includes a book, a film, and a sound recording, Titon documents the importance of oral tradition to the lives of the congregation's members. These studies provide a useful portrait of a folk church in the valley and offer an example of how a church's traditions function in the lives of its members.

The members of the Fellowship Independent Baptist Church value, above all, a feeling of what they identify as "being old-fashioned." "In such an atmosphere," notes Titon, "tradition and the 'old ways' of doing things, the ways their parents and grandparents worshiped, the ways that have come down in oral tradition, are especially prized." The pastor of the church, Brother John Sherfey, sees this old-fashionedness as a hallmark of his church: a portion of one of his sermons demonstrates the high value he places on tradition:

> Now I think in a lot of churches today, and I'm not knocking 'em, brother, they think they're too good, their members thinks they're too good, the pastor thinks he's too good to walk out in a river and baptize 'em. Many of 'em have told me the waters have got so polluted you can't baptize in 'em. Bless God, you know what it is? They've got to have the water warm so they won't get their little legs cold. Amen? Amen, bless the Lord. And it's got to be so nice, and so cozy and all of that, you know, and they've got to build 'em a little pool back here with the heated water. Amen? Praise God, I'm saying we ought to

love God enough to go the way Jesus went. You say, "Preacher it don't matter where it is." Some say, "It don't matter if it's a pond or what it is." It does to me, bless God. Amen? I want it to be running water. I want it be in a river, praise the Lord. Hallelujah, thank God.

You say, "Preacher, you're old-fashioned." I know it. I know that. I'm not arguing that point. I'm old-fashioned and I believe we ought to stay thataway.

Emphasizing further this old-fashionedness, Brother Belvin Hurt, a congregation member and lay preacher, contrasts the church's emphasis on informality and tradition with the services he has observed in other churches: "I been in some [churches] that been so society you could hear a pin drop. And this had to be every jot and tittle right so many words, that clock set, so many words said, and you quit. So many songs done picked out before, and everything that right to the very minute how long it take you to do that, then cut it off. Prayer wrote down exactly how many words to say and cut it off. And [to] stand there like that, and do that, that is not old-fashioned. That is just as dry as a last year's bird nest and just as dry as a Texas wind. And that kind don't do me no good. That don't satisfy me unless I feel the power of the Lord Jesus Christ when I'm preaching and speaking."

For members of this church, tradition clearly plays a central role, and this maintenance of tradition in religion mirrors the adherence to traditional methods of earning a living and family structure. Titon points out that just as the "oral tradition of mountain farming was learned in childhood and youth, to be carried throughout adulthood," the "oral tradition of mountain religion, too, was learned in childhood and youth." Brother Sherfey's sermons reflect the close relationship among family life, earning a living, and religious life. In keeping with the themes of old-fashioned life and tradition, Sherfey often uses examples from his past to provide a clear image for the lesson he hopes to convey to his congregation. Drawing on the past both figuratively and literally, the Fellowship Independent Baptist Church demonstrates the importance of oral tradition to one folk religion currently practiced in the valley.

The Mennonite Church

As noted previously, folklorists have studied folk religions in a variety of ways, and I will not recount them all; however, just as Clements defined the folk church by providing a working definition for others to follow, other scholars have chosen to look at traditional religious groups in different ways. Many studies, for example, explore the beliefs of people who "look like folk," including groups isolated from the mainstream by class, ethnicity, culture, or their own preferences. Providing a clear example of such a community, the Mennonite Church in the Shenandoah Valley demonstrates how a group of religiously like-minded persons can form a cohesive community that has maintained its beliefs for many generations.

A discussion of the Mennonite Church is fraught with difficulty because there are a number of different groups within this larger one, each with their own specific beliefs and outlooks on life. Sociologist Calvin Redekop, himself a Mennonite, suggests, however, that the idea of community is essential to all Mennonites' worlds: "In the Mennonite community model, the community has two spheres: The religious, which centers on congregational life, and the mundane, which focuses on the familial and social community. Thus, the Mennonite community reflects the existence of an in-group, which is identified by a subcultural network of ethnic elements such as a common language (Pennsylvania Dutch) as well as common folk arts, folklore, and folkways, including food. All of these helped create a cohesion and a social system that is still fundamentally derived from the religious tradition." Two relevant factors apply to the topic at hand: the community is based on religious belief, and it maintains traditional aspects of its culture as a part of its daily existence. Redekop sums up this all-encompassing feature, noting, "For Mennonites, the congregation or sacred community has tended to be identical with the social, political, and economic—that is, the secular community."

Redekop and others treat the variety of Mennonite communities in great detail within their studies. This overview, however, begins with a brief background of Mennonite history and then examines how traditions have been maintained within the lives of church members, delineating between the various groups but focusing on the Old Order Mennonites, which form a large valley community, particularly in Rockingham County.

The Mennonite Church was formed originally in Switzerland and takes its name from Menno Simons, a sixteenth-century Anabaptist church reformer. For many years the Mennonites suffered at the hands of state-sanctioned churches throughout Europe because of the Mennonite creed, which included congregational interpretation of Scripture and baptism only of adults on confession of their faith. In addition, members believed in a separation of the church and state, refused to bear arms, and refused to take part in the affairs of government or to swear oaths. These beliefs, along with the Mennonites' plain dress, separated them from mainstream European society.

Mennonite groups eventually migrated throughout Europe, settling in the Netherlands, Germany, Poland, and Ukraine. In America, Germantown, Pennsylvania, became the site of the first permanent Mennonite settlement in 1683. From that time on, Mennonite immigrants continued to arrive in Philadelphia, primarily from Germany and Switzerland, gradually expanding their communities west and south. Mennonites established their first settlement in the Shenandoah Valley around 1727 and by the 1780s were well established in the region.

Since their beginnings in Europe, Mennonites have had a strong agrarian basis, whether out of choice or out of an early desire to remain self-sufficient and outside of society. Mennonites have long been and are today known for their agricultural skills. For example, approximately one-quarter of Virginia's milk comes from Old Order Mennonite dairy farms in Rockingham County. Albert Keim, a history professor and Mennonite, theorizes that the Old Order Mennonite community has continued to grow in the late twentieth century because the Mennonites have large families and are "succeeding wonderfully in keeping their young within the fold, largely because they're working very hard and successfully at appropriate agriculture." The strength of the agricultural community has contributed to the strength of the greater community, including the religious community.

Education, too, takes place within the community, strengthening traditional life and perpetuating its value. Lewis Martin, a harness maker and Old Order Mennonite minister, suggests, "The farm is the best place to raise a family—close to the soil and working together, not separately. Our children go to school through the eighth grade—the rest of their education takes place on the farm for the boys and in the home for our girls." As families grow and farmland becomes more scarce, however, many young people are finding employment elsewhere. Still, their work tends to center around the community and its requirements. Men find work in carpentry and carriage and harness shops, while women make rugs and quilts and bake.

Obviously connected by their religious beliefs, Mennonites have traditionally been united by the bond of ethnicity as well. Their Swiss and German heritage provided them with a common language, and for many years the German language was used within the community and in church services: throughout the eighteenth and most of the nineteenth century, Mennonite services throughout the Shenandoah Valley used the German language. Ministers such as John Weaver (1818–77) and John Geil (1799–1890) were well known for using only German in the Church, and Klaus Wust credits Daniel Showalter (1802–89) with being the last to preach only in that language. By 1880, Virginia ministers preached few services in German, although ministers visiting from Pennsylvania would occasionally treat older congregation members to a sermon in their old tongue. Wust recounts that in 1884, the visiting John Hess delivered an address in

German, which, according to an observer, was "an unknown tongue to many Virginia Mennonites," but two years later, when visitors preached in the Pennsylvania Dutch dialect, they were easily understood.

While it is more widely spoken in Pennsylvania, the Pennsylvania Dutch dialect is still used among some older members of the Old Order Mennonite community in Rockingham County. Informants have told me that they remember their parents (a generation that died mostly in the 1940s and 1950s) speaking only Dutch around the home, although recent studies suggest that contemporary Old Order Mennonites in Virginia are not bilingual. Today, all Virginia Old Order church services are conducted in English.

Although the traditional language of the church may have slipped away, the design of the church building has remained constant. Stephen Scott provides a concise description of the Old Order church, inside and out:

> Old Order Mennonite meetinghouses are plain, white, rectangular, one-story structures with gable roofs. There are several entrances around the building, each used by a different age-gender group (older men, younger men, etc.). The interiors of the meetinghouses are starkly plain; white walls with no decora-

Old Order Mennonite church near Dayton, Rockingham County.

tion of any kind, unvarnished floors, and simple benches with narrow backs.
. . . In Virginia the preachers are positioned at one of the gable ends [and]
there is a low platform for the pulpit. Two small sections of benches on either
side of the pulpit are at right angles to the benches in the main part of the
meetinghouse. These are the so-called "amen corners" reserved for older people. In all Old Order meetinghouses males and females sit separately. There
are also different sections for age groups. In Ontario (Canada) and Virginia all
the horses are tied at open-air hitching rails. Since there is no plumbing inside
the church building there are hand water pumps and outhouses outside.

A final note regarding the Old Order Mennonite church harkens back
to the discussion of the informality of the Baptist church. Unlike the spon-
taneity of the services there, the Virginia Old Order Mennonite Church
maintains the following order of worship:

1. Ministers enter
2. Two hymns
3. Opening sermon
4. Silent prayer
5. Deacon reads Scripture
6. Main sermon
7. Concluding comments from other minister (standing)
8. Audible prayer
9. Closing hymn
10. Announcements
11. Benediction

There is obviously room for variation in this plan; however, the structure
of the lives of Old Order Mennonites is reflected in the service. As Redekop
suggests, the religious community and the secular community clearly blend
together to form one large community that serves church members' needs.
Although they differ vastly in their worship services and lifestyles, the Old
Order Mennonites and the Baptists both value traditional life, whether
identified as old-fashioned or simply as a way of life that has changed very
little over time.

Church of the Brethren (Dunkers)

Baptists and Old Order Mennonites are, of course, not the only religious
groups in the Shenandoah Valley who value tradition. The valley is home
to many denominations and varieties of beliefs. Along with the Mennonites, the Anabaptist group known for many years as the Dunkers and now

called Church of the Brethren displays similar beliefs. This group bears study here because researchers into traditional religions in the Shenandoah Valley will likely find references to it.

Carl F. Bowman, chronicler of the Brethren in America, believes, "While in many ways they were equally as 'peculiar' as the Quakers, Mennonites, and Amish, they have received less attention and have much weaker name recognition than any of these other groups." Perhaps presentations of the other groups in the mass media have done much to increase awareness of these more well-known sects. In terms of the early religious traditions in the valley, however, the Brethren are equally important since they, like the Mennonites, were among the earliest German and Swiss settlers in the region. While their religious heritage derives from the same Anabaptist beliefs as the Mennonites and Amish, the Brethren offer an alternative history. As Bowman puts it, their story is significant because it "is the story of their move beyond plainness."

The Brethren were known as *Dunkers* (sometimes spelled *Dunkards* or *Tunkers*) because of their method of baptism by immersion in water, a tradition that has been maintained. Along with this specific Brethren ritual, several other traditional activities set the group off from other Anabaptists. Perhaps most important of these are the love feast and feet washing, rituals that the Brethren continue to perform.

Nineteenth-century Brethren were continually criticized by other church groups for their literal interpretation of the Bible in regard to baptism—early tracts written by their leaders ardently defend the practice of adult baptism and total immersion in water, a practice that the Brethren believed separated them from similar Anabaptist groups such as the Mennonites and Amish. An early-twentieth-century account of a Dunker baptism re-creates the method and emotion involved in this traditional ritual:

> From the rail-less wooden bridge on which we stood, the water underneath looked cold and uninviting. The current was fairly swift. . . . Involuntarily another shudder shook me. I was glad I wasn't going to be baptized!
>
> A sudden hush fell on the company gathered there about that little stream. Two hundred or so there were of us—men, women and little children. . . . Our eyes focused on the water. A short, spare man of medium height . . . was wading out into the stream. He wore hip boots and a suit of clerical black that was evidently waterproof. His head was bare. In his hand he carried a long broom handle. Carefully he stepped to the center of the narrow creek, feeling the bottom with his broomstick as he went. . . . For a moment his stick tapped briskly. Then, apparently satisfied, he nodded his head and waded back toward shore.
>
> On the bank a tense-faced group awaited him—ten boys and girls, ranging

Reverend Charles Nesselrodt (in water) baptizing a young woman at Bayse, Shenandoah County, 1905. (Courtesy Ethel Dellinger)

in age from twelve to twenty-five. . . . The man with the broomstick joined them. Laying aside his improvised staff, he fell to his knees on a piece of rag carpet spread upon the bank. The others followed. With solemn emphasis, the square-jawed man now raised his voice in earnest prayer. At its conclusion, the little group arose. The man in the hip boots, quietly seizing the arm of one of the boys, walked once more into the stream. His companion's face was white. Involuntarily he blenched as the icy water nipped his ankles, but with manly purpose he continued forward. In the middle of the creek his conductor turned him so he faced down stream, and bade him kneel. The youth obeyed. The water was up to his armpits now. . . . With his hand, the other wet the nape of the boy's neck. Then, while utter silence held those watching from the bridge and bank, he put three solemn questions:

"Do you believe that Jesus Christ is the Son of God and came from Heaven to earth with the soul-saving Word?"

Only the cold lapping of the water and the moaning of the wind broke the little pause that followed. Through chattering teeth, the kneeling applicant replied:

"I do."

"Do you willingly renounce sin and Satan and all his pernicious ways?"

More quickly this time, the youth assented.

"Do you promise to be faithful unto death?"

Again the answer came. The administrator placed his left hand over the face of the kneeling youth, his right at the back of his neck. "Then, with this confession of faith," he announced, "in the presence of God and these witnesses, I baptize you for the remission of sins, in the name of the Father—"

With a single practiced motion, he plunged the youth face forward in the icy current. He came up gasping. Gently the hawk-nosed man smoothed back his dripping hair and waited.

"And the Son—" Again the shivering head and shoulders were immersed. Another pause.

"And the Holy Ghost!" For the third and final time the gesture was repeated. With his hand on the head of his newly baptized charge, the administrator offered a brief prayer. He raised the youth from his knees. Still standing in the water, he extended the right hand of fellowship and planted the kiss of love upon his cheek. Then, leading him to the bank, he turned him over to the square-jawed man. Again the hand of fellowship was offered. Someone stepped forward with a dry coat. He threw it around the young man's shoulders. A new member had been received into the church!

With keen and reverent interest I'd followed the impressive rite from start to finish. So this was a Dunker baptism! . . . "German Baptist Brethren" was their real title, I knew, but like the Quakers, the name Dunker—or Tunker—given originally in derision, had stuck.

The somewhat astonished tone of this account demonstrates the view of many nonmembers. Nevertheless, the passage does provide a unique glimpse of a traditional Brethren baptism.

Referring to other Brethren traditions, Bowman suggests that in the past "feetwashing and the Lord's Supper (unlike communion) were the 'peculiar' elements that distinguished the love feast from typical Protestant liturgy," and they, too, therefore warrant a brief description here. Perhaps the most sacred of the Brethren celebrations, the love feast consists of three parts: washing of feet, the Lord's Supper, and communion. The foot washing began with a hymn and reading of Scripture, followed by the washing, in which two members generally would wash and dry and then exchange roles with others until all members' feet had been washed. Men and women were separated.

Following the washing of feet, the Lord's Supper was served, consisting of bread, beef, and broth. This was not a social occasion but was instead a solemn time for reflection. More hymns were sung, and the tables were cleared and prepared for communion. Following more reading of Scripture, Bowman notes, "the elder greeted the brother next to him; and like wise, forming a chain of unity and brotherly love that was passed all the way around the table and back to the elder that began it. The same action, sometimes called 'passing the peace,' was repeated among the sisters." Finally, communion began with two cups of wine (one for the men and one for the women), which were passed around until everyone had partaken of the drink. The evening concluded with another hymn and prayer.

A brief description of the church buildings and the services rounds out this concise discussion of the Brethren. Groups originally met in members' homes, but by the mid–nineteenth century specific worship buildings known as "plain meetinghouses" were constructed. These simple, one-room structures lacked fancy glass, pulpits, or any kind of ornamentation. For the elders and ministers who were speaking, a single long table was placed in front of and on the same level as the pews. No musical instruments were permitted in the service, although there was much singing, particularly as a group. Choirs and soloists were frowned on. Without hymnals, the verses of the songs were "lined" by one member and then repeated by the congregation to memorized tunes. In general, the services were informal, having, as Bowman states, "no ushers, no acolytes, no offerings, no formal litanies, no worship aids, no special music, no worship themes, no alter calls, and no Holy Communion during the service."

As this overview of the Brethren suggests, the group maintains many traditions but has lost others. Bowman believes that much of this organization's life relies on a shared ethnicity. Members the Brethren Church who are meeting for the first time, he notes, play a sort of name game to see how they are related, often finding a common ancestor or cousin several generations back. Still, despite the value placed on ethnicity, many traditions that once defined the church are now sources of dispute. While many look to the past, in terms of a shared heritage, for example, others are opening the church to other ethnic groups, including African Americans, Hispanics, and Koreans. This broadening necessarily changes traditions within the group. Still, with its strict eighteenth- and nineteenth-century religious traditions, the Brethren Church remains an interesting study in a tradition-oriented church that was among the first in the Shenandoah Valley.

This succinct look at three valley denominations is necessarily limited in its scope. Many other groups that merit study have been left out; however, the Baptists, Mennonites, and Brethren illustrate the importance of tradition to religious groups in the region and suggest the variety of ways that representative groups have responded to the changing conditions of life in the twentieth-century Shenandoah Valley. Old-fashionedness is clearly valued among the groups, although this appreciation is manifested in different ways. The traditions of the first valley settlers remain among these church members; however, the customs have been altered, as all traditions must be, to adjust to contemporary life and its demands.

CHAPTER 6

Folk Medicine and Beliefs

A region's traditional beliefs are often closely tied to its religion. Most residents see no discrepancy between a faith in God and a wise way to heal a sick child or keep away bad luck. Folk medicine, or traditional cures, are those learned primarily through the process of oral tradition, providing an accurate reflection of a community's medical beliefs and practices. Because of this oral quality, many observers consider traditional medicine to be a vestige of the past, no longer current or valid in today's culture. Such, however, is not the case: folklorists, anthropologists, and medical scholars have found that many traditional medicines continue to be used in contemporary society.

Folk medicine can basically be divided into three main categories: household medicine (home remedies), herbalism and other forms of naturopathic healing, and magical medicine. Home remedies can often be made from ingredients found in the home and remain widely used in place of over-the-counter or prescription drugs. Herbs have long been used for healing, and the large number of stores that sell herbs for medicinal purposes prove that many people continue to find these remedies a source of relief from common ailments. Although the idea of healing with magic may seem quaint today, some societies retain a strong tradition of medical magic. All three forms of folk medicine were either found in the Shenandoah Valley in the past or continue to be practiced there.

Home remedies were used in the region from the time of early settlement. Before hospitals and doctors were numerous, rural residents relied on themselves and the oral traditions of their forebears to heal common disorders, and evidence from nineteenth-century journals and personal books demonstrates a wide variety of cures for many human and animal ailments. Demonstrating the assortment of remedies for one illness, the following entries from nineteenth-century Shenandoah Valley personal books provide a sense of the cures commonly used in the valley.

Andrew Hess, born near Waynesboro, Pennsylvania, in 1829, migrated to the valley around 1850, ultimately settling near the Augusta County community of Sangerville. A typical self-sufficient farmer, his handwritten personal book, full of "receipts" for numerous disorders, displays the self-reliance necessary for survival in the rural countryside. For example, he recorded the following three remedies for rheumatism:

Receipt for Rheumatic Drops
take 1 quart of alcohol, 1/4 # gum mush
2 teaspoonful of cayenne pepper
put the above ingredients in a stone jug & put the jug in a hot sand bath for
   3 or 4 days & it is fit for use

Liniment for Rheumatism
olive oil, spirits of camphor and chloroform
of each two ounces
sassafras oil one teaspoonful
first add the oil of sassafras to the olive oil, then the spirits of camphor and
   shake well before putting the chloroform
shake when used keeping it well corked
apply 3 or 4 time a day

For Stiff Joints
Alcohol one pint
gum camphor 2 ounces
neats foot oil 1/2 pint
spirits of turpentine six ounces
oil of juniper 2 ounces
shake the bottle when used and apply 3 time daily

For a cold, Hess could choose from two remedies:

Syrup for Colds
take one hand full of rattle weed root
one hand full of hore hound
2 oz of licker root
1 lb of brown sugar
boil the roots well, then add the sugar & licker juice & 1 pint of good whiskey

Cough Medicine
1 oz olive oil
1 oz paregoric
1 oz fluid extract of licorice

1 oz of chloroform
1 oz glycerin
1 oz extract of lemon
1 lbs white sugar
1 qt water

Hess's book contains more than one hundred recipes for cures, often, as do these examples, containing a mixture of herbs or roots and items available from the local store.

Similarly, George Chrisman Kring, a silversmith from northern Rockingham County, also recorded variations of cures for rheumatism and a cough:

Cure for Rheumatic
take rattle weed roots boil them in five quarts of water down to a gallon
when cold put in one quart of ripe whiskey
drink a dram night and morning
Boil it in a pot that never had grease in it

For a Cough
take one quart of sharp vinegar, one quart water and one handful of hore
    hound, one handful of allicompane roots
boil it down to a quart, then strain it
then put one pint of honey in it
then put it on a slow fire and boil it down to a pint
take a tablespoon full night and day

To Cure Cough
a concoction of the leaves of the pine tree sweetened with loaf sugar to be
freely drank warm when going to bed at night and cold throughout the day

Such helpful remedies were printed in public sources, including newspapers: this cure was preceded by a note reading, "From the Register of 26 July 1840," referring to the *Rockingham Register*.

Along with their own health, valley residents needed to maintain the well-being of their animals. Many cures offered remedies for horse maladies, and Peter Armentrout, a Rockingham County resident at the turn of the nineteenth century, possessed three remedies for treating horse ailments. These cures have been translated from his book, which is written in German.

When there is swelling in a horse, when he cannot walk, boil kidney vetch in water and feed it often for one hour. Do it again for another [hour], and then let him drink as much as he wants but not too much. It will certainly help.

If a horse does not want to eat, stroke his teeth with onion or garlic or make a brew with onions and garlic. Then he will eat. If it doesn't work, do it again.

If a horse has a wound or a bruise, take a handful of viper grass and black root, cut it in small pieces, and boil it in hog grease so that one can smear the brew on the injured part.

Similarly, Dillman Will, of Toms Brook in Shenandoah County, included the following remedies in an 1861 letter to his brothers:

Care for Scratches on Horses
Take equal quantities of the following ingredients viz. salt, soft soap, gun powder, and lard, mix together and apply once or twice a day until a cure is effected. It generally cures in four or five days.

Purging or Scours in Calves
Chalk and gingers, a tablespoonful each, put into the milk of the calf, will cure scours. Stir while the calf is drinking, this keeps the powdered chalk from settling at the bottom of the vessel.

Not only examples of home remedies, these recipes demonstrate a blending of home cures and naturopathic healing because they often combine roots and herbs with other ingredients to produce a cure. This combination is not surprising since naturopathic medicine has undoubtedly been practiced in the valley since Native Americans lived there. Still used today, herbs form a basis for many cures in nearly all societies. An interesting example of the use of herbal healing in the Shenandoah Valley comes from the life of John Kline, a Brethren minister from Rockingham County who tended both spiritually and physically to communities throughout the mid-Atlantic region in the mid–nineteenth century. In a biography of Kline, Benjamin Funk, Kline's protégé, wrote of the minister's use of herbs gathered on his travels, "He procured his remedies in their virgin purity from the mountains, meadows and woods, either in person, with hoe in hand, or through agents whom he employed for the work. Lobelia, Boneset, Pleurisy-Root, Black-Cohosh, Blue-Cohosh, Lady's-slipper, Red Raspberry, Ginseng, Spignet, Black-Root, Seneca-Snake-Root, Gentian, May-Apple, Golden-Rod, and many other roots and herbs were quite familiar to him, not only as they were seen growing in their native mountains, fields and forests, but also as to their medical properties and uses." Funk sprinkles his narrative of traveling with Kline with short anecdotes of time spent looking for herbs. Funk himself apparently was not as zealous in his pursuit of these herbs; he notes on one occasion that while stopping to dig the roots of a goldenseal patch, "We dug up the yellow roots with zest; but being by this time very hungry, I began to fear that we might come across a 'patch' of something else that might still longer delay our return." Perhaps because of his knowledge of the medicinal uses of wild plants and his perseverance in gathering them, Kline was known as a successful doctor throughout the region.

Kline also sought out a plant that many are familiar with today through numerous television advertisements and health food stores—ginseng. Funk, again accompanying his mentor into the mountains, records that "we repaired to the Shenandoah Mountain to procure medicinal herbs. We went up into a very deep and rich hollow, where it looked as if the rays of the sun could hardly penetrate, and soon I saw his face light up with something that evidently pleased him. 'Ah! here it is,' said he. 'What is here?' I asked. 'Don't you see this patch of Ginseng?' he replied. 'Is this Ginseng? It is my first sight of it.'" This passage not only attests to the knowledge of this plant's qualities in the 1830s but also demonstrates the oral tradition involved with valley folk medicine practices. Funk is learning herbal lore not from a textbook but from a teacher literally in the field.

As noted earlier, use of plants and herbs as medicine did not end with the nineteenth century. In 1994, folklorist Kevin Harter interviewed a group of Rockingham County men who still search for ginseng in the mountains. Some of them have also attempted to cultivate ginseng to reap profits from the large global market for this plant that is believed to reduce stress and increase energy. Like Funk, one informant remembered acquiring his knowledge through oral tradition: "Well, I learned about it years ago, back in the late forties. It wasn't much work around at that time, and I'd go to the mountains, and I had an uncle, and he knew what ginseng was, and we would dig it and sell it [in] the Fall of the year, you know. At that time it was around eight dollars a pound—dried ginseng." While describing overnight trips into the mountains to hunt for the plant, the informant also demonstrated how legends can spring up in many different places. Recounting the alacrity of one ginseng hunter, the storyteller laughs, "Some people get carried away with it. One guy found a stalk one time that came up through some rocks, in the crevice. And it wasn't room enough there to dig down and get the root out. And somebody later on went back there with some dynamite and dynamited that rock just for that one stalk! It doesn't make no sense, but he was desperate! . . . They said that was true—I don't know if it was or not." As this anecdote suggests, legends may arise not only from the cures affected by naturopathic means but also from the procurement of the herbs themselves.

The third type of folk medicine, magical, has also been practiced in the valley and often utilizes herbs as a part of the healing process. However, magical medicine relies primarily on verbal charms and ritualized actions that only a healer knows or has the power to use successfully. For example, many people are aware of certain rituals for removing warts, but in some regions "wart doctors" are consulted to alleviate discomfort. In any case, the rituals and charms must be performed properly for a cure to take place.

The Pennsylvania Germans who moved into the Shenandoah Valley were strong believers in the power of magic to heal. Elmer Smith and John Stewart found that this ethnic group had several ideas about the nature of diseases and that each called for a different type of remedy. Smith and Stewart note, "When sickness occurred and a cause for the ailment was apparent, it was thought that the origin was the natural result of either inheritance or contagion. Whenever an understandable cause of a sickness was lacking, it was considered to result from a supernatural origin and was then associated with evil spirits, a spell initiated by human witches or an act of God using an affliction as a punishment or a trial." The latter case, of course, required dramatic measures to alleviate the suffering, and here is where brauche entered in. Brauche (pronounced bra-ka) is an occult practice widely followed by the Germanic people who settled the valley and surrounding regions. The word itself is a dialect word roughly translated as "to use." Another common regional word for this type of healing is *powwowing*, which apparently entered into the language from Algonquin in the seventeenth century. Regardless of the name used, Smith and Stewart found that in the early 1960s there was no shortage of practitioners of this white magic.

Powwowing brings healing back to a discussion of religion, for it is traditional healing of humans and animals based on a belief in the unity of all things—heaven, earth, and all of nature. The diseases sent by an evil force, most often the Devil, require the power of the good forces of nature and religion represented by God, the Trinity, and saints. Thus, many of the incantations used in powwowing incorporate biblical verses and invoke the help of holy personages and saints in warding off illness.

Knowledge of powwowing or brauche is often passed along through oral tradition, but it can never be transferred to a member of the same sex. One informant substantiated this belief, claiming, "I couldn't teach my daughter or granddaughter, they say it won't work if you hand it down to someone in your sex or close kin. The cures won't hold no more." In addition to special knowledge of the charms and rituals, practitioners were most often perceived as having special powers. Often the seventh son in a family was suspected of possessing special powers, as were those who had never known their fathers.

A common ailment often cured by brauche was thrush (also known as thrash), a contagious disease that occurs most often in children, producing a fever and tiny white ulcers in the mouth and on the tongue. One of Smith and Stewart's informants recalled her father curing thrush: "He would go into the stable and get straws from the manure pile. Then take the straw and draw it through the mouth of the person with the thrash three times. While he passed the straw through he said 'strong words' that he said were in the Bible. When he finished he said the 'high words' [Father, Son, and Holy Ghost], and then took the straws and tied a string around them and hung them in back of the stove or next to the chimney. He said that when the straw is dry the thrash will disappear." Another cure, this one for the skin disease erysipelas, or wildfire, employs a special charm along with naturopathics. This informant, from Augusta County, remembered,

> My father taught me to cure for wild fire. You use a red string and a forked prong from a peach tree or witch hazel bush. As you run the red string over the afflicted area you say the words, repeating the operation three times. Then you say:
>   Wild fire, Wild fire, Wild fire,
>   Hee, Hee, Hee!
>   Flee! Flee! Flee!
> Wrap the string around the wood and put it back of the flue at the wood stove.

These two firsthand accounts were recorded in the early 1960s; however, a powwow book found just west of the Shenandoah Valley in Pendleton County, West Virginia, and dating to the eighteenth century confirms that these traditions are deeply seated in the culture of Germans who settled this region. The book, a small folio written in German, contains more than sixty recipes for a variety of illnesses, including animal sickness. Although there is no order to the cures, they may be broken down as follows:

> sickness and disease of human beings
> treatments for dog bite and snakebite
> sickness and disease of animals (horses, cows, mice)
> ways to catch thieves
> ways to keep guns from firing
> bewitching of people and animals
> ways to make a woman tell her secrets
> how to be right at all times
> a blessing for safety at all times
> ways to extinguish a fire
> a magic square

The variety of topics listed not only suggests the types of healing thought to require special powers but also offers insight into other realms where magic might be needed. Consider the benefits of an incantation to "make one right at all times" or to make women tell their secrets.

The following instructions and incantations from the Pendleton County powwow book illustrate the blending of magic, religion, and the natural world in powwow or brauche.

To Stop Blood and Wounds
Blessed be the day when Jesus Christ was born
Blessed be the day when Jesus Christ was born
Blessed be the day when Jesus Christ arose from the dead
These are the holy 3 hours
Thus I cure [name], your blood and cure your wounds
That should never swell or become worse
As much as Martha will never bear another son + + + [signs of the cross]

Another Way to Stop Blood
Three happy hours have come into this world. In the first hour God was born, in the other hour He died. In the third hour He was become part of us. Now I name the 3 happy hours and I put to you [name] so that your limb and the blood heal against damage and wounds + + +

Fever
Walnut tree I come to you. Take the 77 fevers from [name] + +. I am going to insist on this + + +.
One ought to write this on a piece of paper and to go to a walnut tree before sunrise, cut a piece of bark out of it, put the piece of paper in it. Recite the above 3 times and then put the bark back so that the tree will grow together again.

For Arthritis
Take shavings or bark from a linden tree. Cook them. Take a bath in it and make a tea from linden blossoms. It helps.

The book also offers nine recipes for healing animals, including these three.

When a Horse is Tired
When a horse under you gets tired or hurts then relieve nature on a piece of your shirt tail and tie this around the reins of the horse—this ought to help.

To Make a Horse Patient
Against a rebellious horse, call the name of the horse. Be tame and patient when I sit on you—as Jesus Christ was patient + + +.

When the Cow Loses Her Milk
When the cow loses her milk so that it will return. From such a cow take a new bucket of milk, pour it at 3 different times in running water, upward, in the + + + this must be done 3 times, morning evening, and again in the morning.

In a way, the cures and incantations in the Pendleton County powwow book incorporate all types of folk medicine. As the examples demonstrate, reliance on plants and items available in the home mixed with superstition or religion could play a large role in the maintenance of one's spiritual and physical health. It is significant to note the repetition of the number three in these examples as well. That number plays an enormous role in Western culture, and the number's recurrence in this powwow book further demonstrates the traditional quality of the collection. The beliefs collected in the book reflect an ancient understanding of how the world works, and it is significant that although this book was compiled in the eighteenth century, the traditions within it were practiced into the second half of the twentieth. Such an example clearly links Shenandoah Valley folklife with its European origins.

Folk medicine has certainly not died out in the Shenandoah Valley. University students sent off to record traditional life frequently return with at least one cure, and many residents know how to get rid of hiccups or remove warts. One example illustrates well the juxtaposition of folk medicine and modern technology. When interviewed in 1996, a Rockingham County informant who learned from her father how to stop blood proclaimed that she did not need to see the patient to perform the brauche—she simply stopped the bleeding over the telephone.

CHAPTER 7

Fairs and Festivals

Nearly everyone who has spent much time in the Shenandoah Valley has visited a county fair. County fairs conjure up images of quilts and canned fruits mingled with tractor pulls and miniature pig races. One academic described fairs as "local festivals, which have predictable schedules and are marked by expressive public forms such as parades, rituals, and competitions that serve educational, social, economic, and symbolic functions." Fairs, then, offer a microcosm of the community that produces them; as a result, they provide a rich resource for displaying traditional culture.

Agricultural fairs have been held in the valley for more than one hundred years, demonstrating the importance of farming to this rural region. Early fairs, like those throughout the United States, emphasized modernization while maintaining ties to traditional farming techniques. Similarly, like today's fairs, entertainment was also important. Visitors to the 1893 Spring Fair in the Rockingham County city of Harrisonburg were given the choice of listening to a band contest, watching a "match game of base ball," or, if they were interested in education, attending the Farmers' Institute "conducted by leading specialists."

Orra Langhorne, columnist for the *Southern Workman*, visited the first Spring Fair in 1892 and reported that the town "wore a holiday aspect." She continued, "Assembly park was given over for the day to a meeting of the Farmers' Alliance, which was out in force. . . . Machinery of many kinds, much of it in operation, was on exhibition. To the uninitiated it might have been taken for a successful experiment in the co-operative plan of living, of which one hears so much from social philosophers. A steammill was running, laundry and cooking establishments [were] in full operation, tables filled with attractive viands were set—to which all were invited—while enough machines for all sorts of work were scattered about under the spreading trees to inspire the hope that all weary hands could rest and the owners bask in the knowledge that work was 'doing itself.' " As is still the case today, early country fairs presented new ideas to local farmers.

County fairs in the valley also emphasize the interconnections between the traditional past and the present. Exhibits of items such as handcrafted quilts, homegrown canned and fresh fruits and vegetables, and livestock demonstrate the continuity of the valley's traditional life, while the latest air-conditioned John Deere tractors suggest the changes that continually occur in the region's chief business. Joyce Ice sums up the world of the county fair by suggesting that "they have always combined a dual nature with a multiplicity of voices and symbols emphasizing progress and technology while at the same time presenting a nostalgic view of a romanticized rural past. The tensions and contradictions between an impulse for change versus a need for stability, between emerging and ongoing traditions, between various participants and fair audiences, and the relationships of animal and human, of human and machine, of rural and urban—all find expression against the backdrop of the fair."

While contemporary fairs and festivals still emphasize the wonders of modern machinery for both the home and the farm, some events pay hom-

Impromptu discussion at the Page County Heritage Festival, 1994.

age to the old, traditional ways of doing things. Held annually since 1969, the Page County Heritage Festival (separate from the Page County Agricultural and Industrial Fair) celebrates the county's past by opening historic buildings to the public and demonstrating traditional farming techniques and foodways. Featured demonstrations include soap making, quilting, wool spinning, and apple-butter boiling. Similarly, steam- and gas-powered engines exhibit earlier methods of threshing and sawmilling. Traditional crafts have been a part of the festival, too; however, despite the rule that items to be displayed and sold must be handmade, craft pieces often reflect the current popular trend toward cute "country folk art" that has little to do with traditional Shenandoah Valley life. Fortunately, there are exceptions, and traditions such as white oak basket making can be found among the teddy bears and dried flower arrangements that take up space in the exhibit halls.

Like fairs, festivals draw on traditions that are important to a community but often take a more celebratory angle. Like the Page County Heritage Festival, events are organized to call attention to a significant aspect of community life or that of a particular group. Such grassroots festivals occasionally evolve into events designed to attract tourists and consumers from different regions and as such lose some of their local aspects, taking

Making apple butter at the Page County Heritage Festival, 1994.

on the mantle of mass popular culture. In the Shenandoah Valley two such festivals that celebrated important agricultural features were initiated in the first third of the twentieth century, and, while they did base their ideas in traditional occupations of the region, they quickly succumbed to the desire to pull in more tourists.

In 1998, the apple and poultry industries are two of the largest agribusinesses in the valley, and they were important features on the rural landscape as long ago as the 1920s and 1930s. A large portion of these two industries' statewide output came from the valley, and they were an integral part of the community. Along with their official business, the two provided ample ground for traditional activities. Orchards required barrels in which to ship apples, and a tradition of coopering arose. Similarly, turkey farmers required men to raise the flocks and to actually catch the birds, which grazed freely on the range. Such occupational lore, however, was seldom documented, and the stories that have been told of these businesses are those of the owners and entrepreneurs. From these origins grew the Shenandoah Apple Blossom Festival and the Rockingham Turkey Festival, both initiated in the 1920s and 1930s as publicity events.

In 1924, a group of civic leaders from throughout the valley organized "Shenandoah Valley Incorporated," an association designed to increase the tourist flow through the valley and to encourage visitors to stop and contribute to the region's economy. One of this body's first acts was to encourage the creation of a festival that would draw attention to the apple-growing industry, which was prominent throughout the valley. The city of Winchester accepted the challenge and quickly produced the first Shenandoah Apple Blossom Festival in May of that year.

Unlike festivals that celebrate community traditions, however, the Apple Blossom Festival aimed at pageantry, offering a majestic parade, the coronation of "Queen Shenandoah", and a grand pageant presented at the local high school with participants from throughout the valley. With much success and fanfare, the festival was proclaimed just six years later to be as grand and well known as Mardi Gras. Throughout the literature, however, there is little mention of the traditions involved with the apple industry. Foodways in the valley were closely tied to the fruit: sweet and hard apple cider, applejack and brandy, and most importantly apple butter had long been staples of the valley diet. The lore of coopers and stave makers, too, was apparently ignored in the extravaganza. The closest any visitors to the festival would come to the occupational lore of the apple industry was if they piled into one of the private automobiles commandeered for the weekend and visited the orchards themselves. Expecting nearly twenty thousand visitors for the inaugural festival, the organizers sent out a plea for "every car in Winchester, Frederick and Clarke counties which can be spared and

Apple harvesting in Frederick County, c. 1920. (Courtesy Winchester–Frederick County Historical Society)

donated for that day." The committee apparently thought that visitors should see some actual apple blossoms. Except for during World War II, the Shenandoah Apple Blossom Festival has been held annually since 1924 and has grown into a four-day affair that still includes the parade and the crowning of the queen.

Rockingham County's attempt at a major industrial festival met with less success, however. The first Rockingham Turkey Festival was held in September 1939, and it existed for two more years until it was curtailed during World War II. Several subsequent attempts have been made to revive the festival. Like its neighbor down the valley, the Turkey Festival attempted to bring a broader awareness of the importance of the bird. Taking its cue from other festivals, the initial program featured a pageant, aptly entitled "Turkeyrama," that presented the role of the turkey throughout the history of America. From "The Turkey in Tom Tom Days" to "The Turkey Comes to Life," the show portrayed how the turkey became a valuable and important participant in the life of the United States as well as the county.

Again, like the Apple Blossom Festival, the Turkey Festival celebrated

Bronze turkeys on the range in Rockingham County, c. 1940. (Courtesy Harrisonburg-Rockingham Historical Society)

the industry but never touched on the traditional life that maintained it. The final "episode" of the Turkeyrama, for example, featured the turkey drive, a representation of farmers driving their birds to market in flocks. Like cattlemen, turkey farmers found the drive the easiest way to transport their animals, and many stories and traditional aspects of this annual event undoubtedly were never brought to the public's attention. By the second year of the festival, new events were added, including "turkey throws" on Court Square and a firemen's and mummers' parade. The events would not be complete without the coronation of Queen Rockingham.

It is ironic, perhaps, that a more recent festival demonstrates more signs of a true event held to educate and celebrate a culture. The Latin American Encounter, first held in 1994, was organized in Rockingham County by Hispanics, faculty members from Eastern Mennonite University, and members of the Catholic and Mennonite Churches. The festival organizers sought to broaden the local community's knowledge of Hispanic culture by providing Anglos an opportunity to learn about different Latin American cultures, thereby decreasing feelings of distrust between some whites and Hispanics. Dismayed by public reaction and police actions following the April 1994 shooting of a Mexican immigrant in Harrisonburg, Hispanic leaders and others organized the festival to enlighten the community about the rich Hispanic culture and to celebrate Hispanic cultural contributions to the region.

Featuring music, food, and cultural displays from eight Latin American countries, the First Latin American Encounter (Primer Encuentro) was held in Harrisonburg in October 1994. Repeated annually for three years, the festival highlighted the valley's growing Hispanic community and offered area residents the chance to meet individuals and experience their traditions. The music, food, and folk arts of these groups were on display, and although there was initially racist reaction to the event, the festival proceeded. About two hundred people from many ethnic groups attended the First Latin American Encounter.

Shenandoah Valley fairs and festivals, both historic and recent, offer glimpses of what the community believes is important to celebrate. Agricultural fairs provide a venue for farmers and homemakers to show off the fruits of their labor and for displaying the latest innovative techniques in the field. Festivals often commemorate the past and the present both to remind residents of the value of traditions and to explain different cultures to other groups within the region. The Shenandoah Valley's celebrations represent a microcosm of the traditional life found there.

PART Four

Material Culture

The Shenandoah Valley has a rich legacy of traditional crafts and arts, many of which continue to be maintained today. The indelible influence of the Germans, Swiss, and Scots-Irish remains evident in both historic and contemporary examples of the region's folk art, while the mark of popular culture from outside the valley is also unmistakable. When the valley was settled in the eighteenth century, subsistence farming was the norm, and residents crafted the items they needed to survive. This trend continued until the middle of the nineteenth century, when improved transportation and communications with the rest of the nation led to changes in the ways traditional communities relied on themselves and others nearby. By the 1870s many craftsmen in the Shenandoah Valley were affected not only by their Pennsylvania neighbors but by companies in the Midwest and Northeast.

Historically, however, traditional crafts included metalworking, ceramics, gunsmithing, and woodworking (including cabinetmaking, carpentry, and basketry). Some of these crafts have been maintained, while others, no longer essential, have been replaced by mass-production techniques. German schoolteachers no longer artfully create fraktur to mark important rites of passage for community members, and potters no longer produce wares required for daily chores and food preservation. Conversely, basket makers, quilters, furniture makers, and others are still at work, in some cases utilizing ideas and decorative motifs that have been in the valley for hundreds of years.

Perhaps more tenacious than the crafts are valley foodways. Early European immigrants maintained many Old World traditions after arriving in

America, and potatoes, cabbage, and pork today remain important parts of the valley diet. Traditional meals often mark holidays and special gatherings, such as the hog butchering that continues to bring family members together as each one pitches in on that arduous task. Seldom found on modern restaurant menus, traditional dishes such as ham pot pie are served at fund-raising dinners, where they are sure to bring a crowd.

Unlike food, buildings will often last for centuries, and many examples of early Shenandoah Valley architecture remain extant. It is safe to say that traditional building methods and house types are all but gone now, although contemporary stonemasons carry on that craft as they maintain existing stone houses and fences. The historic buildings that remain demonstrate the ethnicity of their builders while attesting to the fact that acculturation took place in many ways, including methods of house construction and selection of a building plan.

CHAPTER 8

Folk Art and Craft

As in all cultures, Shenandoah Valley folk art exists within the realm of traditional crafts. The decoration of useful, everyday items has long been a way to lighten the load of the hard work required to subsist on farms or toil in the city. In all cases, folk art reflects the beliefs and acceptable motifs of the community that produces it. Folklorist John Michael Vlach asserts, "The essential characteristics of folk things stem from their communal nature. Because they are shared expressions they are not unique but typical and even commonplace; they are not usually monumental but ordinary and familiar; they are not singular but precedented, formulaic, and duplicated; they are not the product of a lone instant but are repeated continuously." This communal nature can be found in all traditional items constructed in the valley. From Germanic birth certificates to hand-built rifles, the stamp of valley craftspeople and artists is evident.

Fraktur

Still found tucked in Bibles and attached inside the lids of hand-built chests, fraktur paintings are among the earliest examples of folk art in the Shenandoah Valley. The term *fraktur* refers to the illuminated manuscripts that were created in the valley and other primarily German areas of the East Coast to observe births, baptisms, or marriages or as house blessings, bookplates, and other commemorative documents. Always highly decorated, fraktur reflects a direct cultural link to medieval calligraphy coupled with the traditional decorative motifs found throughout the Pennsylvania culture region and thus the Shenandoah Valley. The colorful paintings often include tulips, pomegranates, hearts, distelfinks, and parrots. Seldom signing their work, Shenandoah Valley artists were productive from around 1790 until the 1820s, although later examples are known.

Produced primarily by schoolmasters and ministers, fraktur was mainly the product of Lutheran and Reformed Church schools. Essentially the artistic spokespersons for a community, schoolteachers introduced students to music, poetry, and drawing, in which fraktur played a major role. The inscriptions on fraktur varied according to type; however, most emphasized the community's religious beliefs. There are a variety of types of fraktur, including *vorschriften*, title pages to copy books, rewards for merit, or bookplates, and *taufschein*, which are birth and baptismal commemorations. The latter were primarily rendered by Lutherans or Reformed Church members, not members of the Anabaptist Mennonites and Brethren sects, which do not practice infant baptism. The Anabaptist groups did, however, produce *vorschriften*. Although to a lesser extent than their neighbors in Pennsylvania, residents of the Shenandoah Valley created impressive fraktur that can be found in collections throughout the region.

Despite the relative anonymity of Virginia's fraktur artists, several did

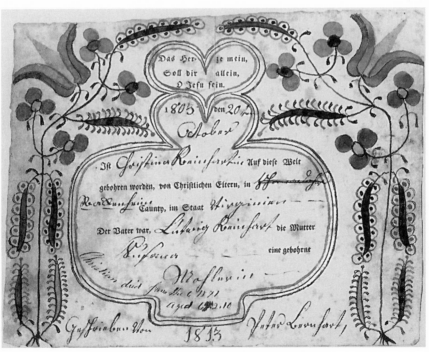

Fraktur by Peter Bernhart, 1813. (Courtesy Glenn Cordell)

sign their works, and others have been narrowed down to a geographic area. One of the most prolific of these artists was Peter Bernhart, a Rockingham County schoolteacher and post rider whose works stretch from Frederick to Augusta County. Bernhart nearly always included not only his name but also the date on which he made the fraktur; his work spans the period 1796–1819. Although the art in his pieces is often crudely executed, the works are colorful and provide fine examples of typical Shenandoah Valley frakturs.

Bernhart's work also demonstrates the close ties that held members of different crafts together. Many of his works were completed on blanks—forms with general information included but with spaces left for specific facts—produced for him by local printers, most often the Henkel Press in New Market or Lawrence Wartmann of Harrisonburg. Bernhart apparently carried these forms with him on his routes; when called on to provide a certificate, he simply filled in the significant information and decorated the area around the printing. Many examples of his fraktur demonstrate this method of production.

Another well-represented artist has never been identified by name but is known simply as the Stony Creek artist after the large amount of his work found near that community in the vicinity of Edinburg in Shenandoah County. Working in the same time period as Bernhart, the Stony Creek artist created fraktur that are recognized by their depiction of a cherub beneath a drawn-back curtain, with the text usually contained within a heart. This artist produced works in both German and English.

Metalworking

Unlike fraktur, which often commemorated special events, metalworkers' products were designed to meet the wear and tear of everyday use. Blacksmiths, gunsmiths, and ironmasters produced functional pieces that they decorated with well-known motifs to relieve some of the arduousness of daily chores. The creativity of early regional blacksmiths can be found on trivets, spatulas, skimmers, forks, and other utensils, always functional works that displayed the craftsman's artistic ability. Hinges for blanket chests and doors also featured innovative designs that enabled the smith to show off his abilities as both craftsman and artist. Today the craft continues to be practiced, primarily by farmers who occasionally need to fix up some bit of metal around their farm. One southern Augusta County man, standing next to his anvil, refused to accept the mantle "blacksmith." "I'm just a jackleg," he said, adding, "I can't do nothing fancy." Of course, many craftsmen before him undoubtedly uttered the same modest words.

Fraktur by the Stony Creek artist, c. 1806. (Courtesy Harrisonburg-Rockingham Historical Society)

Contemporary gunsmiths, too, no longer carry on traditions passed down through time in oral tradition, but they do offer skillful replicas of the once ubiquitous long rifle that played an important role in the subsistence of Shenandoah Valley settlers. Often referred to as Kentucky or Pennsylvania rifles, these firearms were artfully produced by numerous gunsmiths throughout the Shenandoah Valley from the late eighteenth century through the first half of the nineteenth century. Well over fifty gunsmiths offered their pieces for sale throughout the region, and existing examples testify to the quality of their craftsmanship and artistry. Like other works of folk art, the long rifle first served the need for a functional tool, but the carved and engraved designs on the stocks and patch boxes leave no doubt that these men were very conscious of the accepted artistic motifs in the region. Rifles from the valley exhibit such traditional figures as hearts, acorns, and stars, and their stocks were often carved from curly maple, adding another decorative feature to the piece.

Detail of rifle built by Alexander McGilvray, c. 1840. (Courtesy Harrisonburg-Rockingham Historical Society)

While Shenandoah Valley gunsmiths produced distinctive artistic designs, the knowledge of how to build firearms migrated south from Pennsylvania, like many of the region's other traditions. For example, Rockingham County gunsmith George Sites (1771–c. 1850) appears to have had some training in the shop of Hanover, Pennsylvania, master George Schroyer near the end of the eighteenth century. After striking out on his own, Sites became the master of his own apprentices and trained, among others, his son, William. One of Sites's nephews, John P. Sites of Botetourt County, Virginia, also learned the art of gunsmithing, eventually moving to Missouri in 1834. His craft was passed along to his son, John Jr., who continued to build rifles until the late nineteenth century, perpetuating a family tradition from Pennsylvania to the Midwest.

Ceramics

Another indispensable craft was ceramic production, and, like the blacksmith, the potter specialized in creating necessary everyday items. In the years before glass canning jars found their way into most homes, the products of an area potter were necessary for survival. Valley residents preserved meat in stoneware and earthenware jars, put up their apple butter in crocks each autumn, and placed their milk in ceramic pans every day. The image of a southern mountaineer with a jug full of moonshine slung over his shoulder has become cliché; however, jugs were a large part of the traditional potter's repertoire, and whether they held liquor or liniment, they played an important role.

Like other traditional valley craftsmen, potters stepped across the line of creating purely functional work and decorated their pieces. For instance, the normally dreary gray of stoneware was dressed up with bright flowers applied in cobalt blue, and some earthenware pieces were turned in forms that rank among the most graceful examples of Shenandoah Valley folk art. Valley potters numbered in the hundreds in the nineteenth century, and many were highly talented, if unrecognized, artists. Today, decorated and formally attractive ceramics of the eighteenth and nineteenth centuries are highly prized by collectors of American folk art throughout the world.

Of course, not every piece of pottery was decorated since doing so added an extra, unnecessary step to the process. The Rockingham County potter Emanuel Suter, for instance, while a talented artist, largely abandoned the practice of applying decoration by the 1880s as he sought to meet a growing

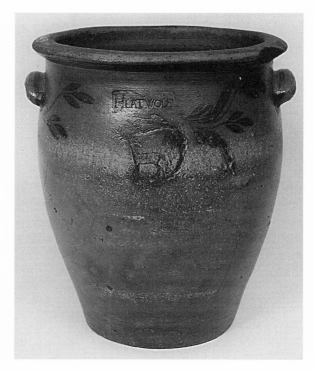

Stoneware crock made by John D. Heatwole, 1850s. (Courtesy Eastern Mennonite University)

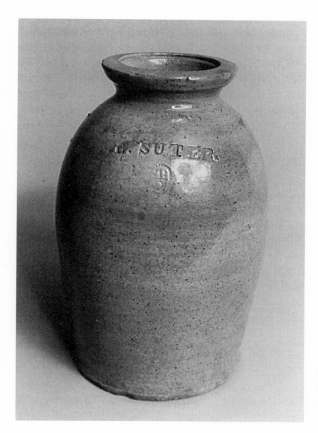

Earthenware jar made
by Emanuel Suter,
1860s. (Courtesy Brook
Levan)

market for his wares. Conversely, his cousin, John D. Heatwole, created
some of the most highly decorated pieces of the area. Like Suter and Heatwole, other valley potters maintained or abandoned certain traditions as
they saw prudent. Several families, most notably the Bells, produced numerous generations of potters, and with each successive change of person-
nel came a change in style. Still, basic methods and designs were preserved
until the turn of the twentieth century, when improved methods of food
preservation replaced traditional pottery.

Cabinetmaking and Basket Making

Many other craft traditions existed in the Shenandoah Valley in the eighteenth and nineteenth centuries, but as transportation to the region in-

creased, customers became aware of national styles and began to prefer those designs to those that were ethnically and community based. Although the late nineteenth century witnessed a nationalization of valley tastes, many traditional craftsmen continued to practice their trade, making concessions to the changes in customer tastes while maintaining the high standards that both they and their customers expected of their work.

Perhaps the best example of this is the work of the Theis brothers, cabinetmakers in the central Shenandoah Valley. Although they emigrated from Germany separately in the 1850s, brothers Christian and Henry Theis eventually set themselves up as cabinetmakers in the Shenandoah County town of New Market. Both served in the Confederate forces during the Civil War, returning to reopen their shop following the conflict. They built all types of furniture and provided the town with coffins and undertaking services as well. Prompted by ill health to sell his interests, Christian turned the business over to his brother in 1889, and Henry remained active in cabinetmaking until his death in 1929.

Advertisements following the Civil War clearly demonstrate that the Theis brothers understood where their main competition lay—not with neighboring shops, but with manufacturers in cities now easily accessible by rail. In 1869 Christian Theis posted the following advertisement in a local newspaper:

Old things have passed away
All things have become new.
Greater inducements than ever to my old friends—
Read the following, and consult your own interests—
Come and compare prices,
Ye who desire furniture of all descriptions,
As I am determined to sell at less than Baltimore.

As the century unfolded, the Theis's furniture took on the look of late-nineteenth-century popular styles, reflecting mass taste at the time. Still, the brothers created their pieces with the quality craftsmanship to which their customers were accustomed, and their business flourished. Other cabinetmakers made this shift, too, and many craftsmen certainly found that as the nineteenth century progressed, they were facing new economic threats from outside their community. As the community's taste became more homogenized, traditional arts began to dwindle until they became less the norm and more often the exception.

Traditional crafts, however, did not cease in the face of these new challenges: they were adapted, and traditional craftsmen today continue to produce excellent examples of valley folk objects. Braxton Theis, grandson of Henry, followed his father and grandfather into the undertaking business and continues to build furniture with his grandfather's tools. Similarly, descendants of Daniel Suter (1808–73), an 1826 Swiss immigrant to the valley and a cabinetmaker, continue to build furniture in Rockingham County. Now, six generations later, a different Daniel Suter directs valley craftsmen at the Suter's Handcrafted Furniture shop, which was founded by the elder Daniel Suter's grandson, Peter, in the early twentieth century.

Family craft traditions such as these are not difficult to find in the valley in the late twentieth century, although one must be careful not to confuse the true bearers of traditions with the many revivalists capitalizing on current popular trends. Rug weavers, quilters, and blacksmiths, for example, produce crafted folk art items daily, and some still make a living in these traditional occupations, while others supplement more conventional sources of income.

One of the most fascinating examples of the long-term survival of a craft is the Shenandoah Valley's white oak basket-making tradition. For more than a century and a half, descendants of the same family, the Nicholsons, have been producing baskets in the region, first in the Blue Ridge Mountains and then in the valley and the Piedmont. In a comprehensive essay on the origins of this tradition, Nancy J. Martin-Perdue recorded that the family first began to build baskets for neighbors in the early nineteenth century and that members of the extended family carried the tradition beyond the confines of the hollows of the Blue Ridge. Descendants of these original Nicholsons—members of the Cook, Nicholas, Nichols, Price, and Turner families—today continue to build according to the old ways.

Whereas before the 1920s most baskets were made for use on the small farms that filled the valley, by the time the automobile became a means of pleasure travel, basket makers realized that they could sell their work to tourists and make more money than was possible working on a farm. In 1968, William Cody Cook, a descendent of the Nicholson clan, recalled his start in basket making: "It was way back there in the deepest of the depression, and times were hard. We were already married, and I was about twenty-five years old. I made our living by farm work in our neighborhood, earning a dollar a day—six dollars a week. So we turned to baskets. We'd never made one before in our lives. . . . In four days we made nine dollars, selling baskets to our neighbors. I never went back to farm work." It is interesting to observe that although they had been around family basket makers for most of their lives, neither Cook nor his wife, Lucy (also descended from the Nicholsons), had ever made baskets before this time.

Other members of the family, based largely in Page County at that time, also realized that basket making was a way to earn money during hard times. Sam Price, whose wife, Rose, was Cook's sister, taught his entire family to make baskets; a photograph from the 1920s shows the group posed by the highway leading to the Blue Ridge Mountains just east of the town of Luray. Jesse Price, the youngest son in the picture, still builds baskets on the eve of the twenty-first century, and his brother, Elmer, was widely recognized as a fine basket maker prior to his death in 1994.

Still, problems threaten the continuity of this important tradition. To grasp the significance of these threats, however, it is first necessary to understand the method of building a white oak basket. Although it may not be obvious, the process begins with the trees themselves. Basket makers first scour the forests around their homes for "sticks," straight white oaks with a diameter of six to ten inches. After cutting down several trees, the basket makers begin the process by splitting one in quarters, carefully pulling it apart until it is eventually worked down into the weavers and ribs required to fashion useful, attractive baskets. Many of these craftspeople believe that the skill of basket making lies in these preparatory steps. Basket maker Bill Cook once remarked, "Anyone can weave a basket, it's getting out the materials that's the hard part." Anyone who has ever attempted to weave a basket will recognize the overstatement in Cook's comment; however, he makes a valid point. The knowledge of how to select a tree and then split it down into thin, pliable strips goes beyond most people's com-

Family of Sam and Rose Price selling baskets at a roadside stand in Page County, 1920s. (Courtesy Harrisonburg-Rockingham Historical Society)

mon knowledge. The necessity of having such specialized knowledge to master this craft further demonstrates the folk nature of the tradition; it has been passed down for generations within this extensive family, always through oral tradition.

Many basket makers with whom I have talked fear the disappearance of this centuries-old tradition, however, as they increasingly face problems in gaining access to usable white oak trees. Several factors—both natural and man-made—have contributed to this obstacle. Landowners' reluctance to part with healthy trees and a National Forest policy that prohibits the cutting of live trees on its property combined with the devastation of the oaks by air pollution and gypsy moths have dramatically limited basket makers' chances of finding usable trees, the essential raw material for their art.

None of the valley's traditional basket makers own of tracts of wooded land, so they must rely on others to sell them trees. While craftspeople must have healthy trees, many landowners are reluctant to give up young ones, preferring instead to let them grow so that they will fetch a higher price at the lumber mill. Although the thinning of a few trees so that others can grow straighter is a sound practice, many basket makers face a stone wall when they approach landowners about cutting a few trees. Gregory Nicholas, who has built baskets with his father, Ernest, for many years, suggests, "Maybe if some of the people really knew the tradition of the

Bill Cook with a variety of white oak baskets.

basket and were really interested in keeping the tradition going, they might be a little more considerate and thoughtful about giving up a few of their trees."

Furthermore, some of the valley's wooded acres are located within the National Forest system. Ernest Nicholas recalls that in the past, the federal government worked closely with basket makers, allowing them to cut trees from National Forest lands: "Years ago, my dad used to buy [white oak] off of them. These men from the Forest Service would come and go with him and he would mark these trees with a little paint or something and he would pay them so much a stick [tree]. He could go in and cut this wood as he needed it, you know. It would be a good thing—I wish it would be that way now, but no way they'll let you cut anything green." Nicholas and other basket makers lament the fact that this policy changed in the 1950s, pointing out that selective cutting was more responsible forest management than the clear cutting that currently takes place.

Ernest Nicholas.

Air pollution places a further burden on the basket-making tradition. Shenandoah National Park, located in the Blue Ridge Mountains, has reported that more than two-thirds of the visibility impairment from its mountain overlooks is the result of "human-caused pollution," primarily from "coal-fired power generating facilities" in the Ohio River basin. As trees are stunted by the valley's less pure air, landowners become more reluctant to part with trees, increasing the problems in finding and accessing healthy trees.

Perhaps the most devastating problem facing basket makers is a natural one, the gypsy moth. In 1981 alone the insect defoliated nearly thirteen million forested acres, primarily white oaks. This threat led the late Elmer Price, a basket maker for nearly seventy years, to lament in 1990, "If something don't happen within four or five years, there won't be any white oaks left." Fortunately, Price's prediction has not come true; however, the gypsy moth, introduced to the United States in the early twentieth century in an effort to increase silk production, continues to destroy large areas of white oak trees.

This look at basket making raises points that are relevant to most of the region's crafts: throughout the years, threats have arisen from a number of sources, primarily increasing technology. Furniture makers certainly experienced pressure from outside the region as they attempted to maintain their quality work in the face of cheaper prices and changing national tastes. Potters, too, found that the call for their wares decreased as the nineteenth century progressed. The once-thriving traditional industry eventually succumbed, and the potteries closed their doors. Still, as the longevity of the basket tradition suggests, folk items—crafts and arts—continue to be produced in the Shenandoah Valley, presenting contemporary patrons the same quality that was offered to their ancestors.

CHAPTER 9

Architecture

Folklorist Henry Glassie's statement that "Buildings, like poems and rituals, realize culture" suggests that built structures can be read like texts, offering meaning to those who build or use them as well as to others who wish to learn from them. Glassie's pronouncement holds true in the Shenandoah Valley: traditional buildings tell the story of the migration of different groups of people and how they organized their lives according to tradition and changed them as new cultural choices presented themselves. The structures tell of a blending as time moved forward.

Explaining the value of exploring the meaning of traditional, or vernacular, buildings, Glassie eloquently maintains his analogy: "The plain, uncluttered form of the vernacular building is the artful external presentation of its internal idea. The aesthetic of the vernacular building is not ornate but logical. It approximates prose more than poetry. As fine prose becomes transparent to let its ideas shine through (in contrast to poetry in which the words draw attention to themselves), the facade of a vernacular building offers little excitement or resistance and always enables the viewer to predict with some assurance the plan within." The valley's houses, barns, and other outbuildings tend to look similar and in many instances even nearly identical; however, as Glassie suggests, this is not the result of a lack of imagination but is instead a marker of culture. Houses built of log or stone in three-room plans reflect the builders' German ancestry, just as frame and log two-room structures show the influence of the English who moved west from the coast and the Scots-Irish who, like the Germans, migrated out of Pennsylvania into the mountains and hollows of the Shenandoah region.

As Germans (including the Swiss) migrated from Pennsylvania into the valley in the eighteenth century, the built environment began to take on the appearance of these new Americans' homelands. The diversity of their backgrounds, which included many different parts of Europe's Germanic culture region, however, did lead to some variation in building designs in America and certainly produced a distinct difference from the English who had already established themselves in Pennsylvania.

The type of eighteenth-century Germanic house now most often found standing in the valley is of the basic three-room plan known as a *flurküchenhaus* or *ernhaus*. This house type features direct entry into a spacious kitchen with another large room, or *stube*, on the opposite side of a massive central chimney. There is often a small sleeping chamber behind the *stube* and a full second story with more sleeping and storage space. The facades of these houses are necessarily off-center, since entrance is gained to one side of the house. The exteriors of these houses uphold Glassie's observation that vernacular buildings often indicate their interior plans and thus the ethnicity of the builders.

Germanic houses in the Valley were usually built of stone or logs, although the latter method was not a part of the cultural baggage of the earliest immigrants. Stone houses were built in the Rhenish regions and continued to be built in America; however, the time and labor-saving method of horizontal log construction quickly caught on among this group, and many of the existing valley homes from this period are built of logs.

Edward A. Chappell, an architectural historian who has studied extensively Germanic building techniques in the United States, has asserted that in America, including the Shenandoah Valley, "around the end of the eighteenth century dramatic changes took place, reflecting powerful acculturative pressures. For perhaps a generation, essential aspects of the old forms and structures were retained but combined in ways that emphasized exterior symmetry and allowed the removal of work functions from the main floor." In other words, as second-generation Germans in the valley built their own houses, the structures began to show signs of a blending of cultures. While floor plans may have maintained the same traditional three-room arrangement, symmetry was produced by building the house with two front doors. Thus, the exterior of the house would look more like a central passage I-house. This house type, with its door in the middle of the facade and an equal number of windows on either side, had become the most popular form in the region by the mid–nineteenth century. Once-immigrant families were becoming Americanized, and the houses they built began to demonstrate this phenomenon. Houses with two front doors continue to stand in some sections of the valley in the late twentieth century.

The Scots-Irish, like the Germans, brought to the valley a distinctive house type that similarly reflects a melding of other traditions. Like the

Sites house, a stone *flurküchenhaus*, Rockingham County. (Courtesy David Edwards)

German plan, the Irish plan featured a door that opened directly into the room with the hearth, a welcome sight to any visitor seeking warmth and hospitality. Smaller than the German plan, however, the house contained only one smaller room off of this main, heated room. With some modification, this two-room plan became the basis of that symbol of American frontier spirit, the log cabin.

The English, too, played a role in adapting this design—known as a hall-and-parlor plan because of its two-room arrangement—to the valley. The English also deserve credit for raising the hall-and-parlor to two stories, producing the previously mentioned I-house. Often thought to have gained its name due to the fact that from the gable end it looks like a capital *I*, the I-house is basically two rooms side by side with two rooms on top of them. These houses initially did not have central hallways; however, as the nineteenth century progressed, more and more I-houses took on a well-balanced appearance, featuring a central doorway usually flanked by one or two windows. Still one of the most common house types in the Shenandoah Valley today, I-houses were constructed of frame, brick, log, and stone.

In the second half of the nineteenth century, as the building of ethnic

Lincoln homestead, a brick I-house, Rockingham County. (Courtesy David Edwards)

house types dwindled and the I-house form became more and more prevalent, alterations to the traditional plan began to occur. These changes usually took the form of an ell addition off of the back of the house. These rectangular expansions, built at right angles to the houses, often included a dining room as well as a kitchen. Side porches eventually were added to the design as work spaces began to spread throughout the house and into buildings built specifically for activities such as washing. The ell addition with side porches contributed a final touch to the typical late-nineteenth-century Shenandoah Valley house.

While old houses on the valley landscape continue to reflect the ethnicity of the original builders, the region's single most recognizable architectural feature is the large forebay barn. Identifiable by its overhanging front and sloping bridge in the back, this massive structure, essential to working farms throughout the nineteenth and twentieth centuries, often continues to serve its original function, providing shelter for animals as well as storage for machinery, hay, and straw.

The origins of this barn type lie in Switzerland, where farmers built

Forebay barn, Augusta County.

structures into the sides of hills to provide easy access to the second level. Brought to Pennsylvania in the eighteenth century, the barn quickly caught on as a functional farm building as the idea spread from farmer to farmer. Migrating south, Germans, Swiss, and Scots-Irish carried the concept of the forebay bank barn with them, eventually introducing the idea to the Shenandoah Valley. Often known as Pennsylvania barns, these structures visually tie the valley to its cultural hearth, southeastern Pennsylvania.

During the Civil War, General Philip Sheridan sought to demoralize the valley's residents and instructed his men to burn every barn that they saw, a testament to both the barns' essential function and their symbolic value as indicators of a flourishing agricultural community. A drive through the valley today reveals that the tradition was maintained, however, as many barns were summarily rebuilt following the war. Attesting to the quality of the design, forebay bank barns were built in the valley well into the twentieth century, as this 1937 newspaper item demonstrates: "An old-fashioned barn raising was held Wednesday on the C. E. Judd farm, five miles west of Harrisonburg. . . . Following an old time custom, 45 men volunteered their services free of charge in spite of the busy season for farmers. The structure

Augusta County homestead with I-house and forebay barn, 1880s. (Courtesy Harrisonburg-Rockingham Historical Society)

... went together without a misfit. ... With practically all the heavy frame in place by 12 o'clock the army of laborers were called to a great picnic dinner held under a spreading cottonwood tree near the structure."

These architectural features have combined to make up the Shenandoah Valley's rich traditional built environment. Germanic and Celtic, Pennsylvanian and Virginian combined to produce an amalgam of log, stone, and frame construction that makes the region distinctive architecturally. Similarly, an accompanying blending of cultural traditions occurred in the nineteenth century, producing what may be called the American farm. Concepts from the different cultures that arrived here in the eighteenth century were adapted on the frontier to produce a uniquely American design. The Irish tradition of single-family farms apart from others, the Swiss forebay bank barn, and other notions produced American and more specifically Shenandoah Valley patterns. Such a landscape signals, as Glassie suggests, a pattern "attributable less to the retention of Old World ideas than to the flexible, synthetic spirit of the frontier."

Valley barn raising, c. 1900. (Courtesy Harrisonburg-Rockingham Historical Society)

Foodways

Like music, tales, buildings, or any other aspect of traditional life examined in this book, food communicates culture. Foods are, in many ways, such everyday items that they often receive little thought. Many foods are certainly nationally and even internationally consumed and have no traditional aspects left; fast-food chains, for example, do not reflect regional cultures but instead betoken American mass culture. Conversely, however, most regions of the United States do maintain certain food traditions. Use of the term *foodways* takes a discussion beyond the food itself and looks at how foods intersect with culture. When are certain foods eaten? Who prepares them? Are there special meals for special occasions? Answers to such questions reveal much about the culture toward which they are aimed. Social aspects of traditional cultures are often studied by examining the ways that foods are used in a variety of gatherings.

Similarly, although foodways are often grouped with material culture (as they are here), they connect to many other aspects of traditional life. For example, pottery was an essential part of food preservation in the nineteenth century; local blacksmiths fashioned useful and artful utensils; and the genres of folk narrative, folk song, belief and custom, and even architecture often feature food-based aspects. In some ways foodways can be seen as an all-encompassing way of studying traditional cultures. This chapter examines two aspects of foodways in the Shenandoah Valley. One example, hog butchering, offers insights into food production, while the other, fundraising foods, provides a look at consumption of traditional foods and their social aspects within the region.

Hogs have long been a source of meat in the Shenandoah Valley. Early farmers let the animals roam wild on their land and butchered them in the fall or winter. Older valley residents recall butchering day with fondness,

Corn shucking brings a Shenandoah Valley community together, late nineteenth century. (Courtesy Harrisonburg-Rockingham Historical Society)

remembering a day of activity spent away from school. Even today, many families still butcher a hog or two, using the occasion to obtain good food for the coming year and as a way of bringing family and neighbors together. Often, like the barn raising described earlier, the effort is a community affair, with neighbors helping neighbors and enjoying a day spent together.

As in the past, butchering day begins early, before the sun rises. Men usually slaughter the hogs, slicing their throats so they will bleed (hence the folk expression "bleeding like a stuck pig"). The hog is then scalded to clean the hide and loosen its bristles, which are then scraped off before the animal is suspended on a tripod or horizontal bar. Next, the head is removed, a crew sets about cleaning and cutting it up, and the animal is eviscerated. Organs such as the liver, kidneys, brain, and heart are set aside as ingredients for specific dishes. Many people consider these parts delicacies—pudding, ponhoss (a mixture of meat scraps, broth, and cornmeal), scrapple, and souse are also produced from various parts of the hog. While this process is taking place, the carcass is cut apart and set on the butchering table, where the hams, tenderloin, side meat, and other sections are divided. With chunks of skin boiling and awaiting the lard press, intestines are cleaned and scraped, making them ready to be filled with the spicy sausage that will soon be ground. The butchering area is a busy place, with the crew members working diligently at their assigned tasks.

Another traditional aspect of the day is the noon meal, which is often provided by the host family if the butchering involves neighbors. A few pieces of the freshly butchered hog are occasionally prepared, but easier meals that can be prepared ahead of time are often served. Whether the day involves family only or includes friends, this meal is seen as an important part of the event. It offers a time for everyone to rest and discuss the day: people have been too absorbed in their tasks to enjoy each other's company.

Butchering day is significant not only as a day for providing meat for the year but also in regard to the ritual it represents. In contemporary society, the job could be easily handled by a custom butcher; however, many fami-

Father and son, Byard and Allen Early, eviscerate a hog, 1993.

lies look forward to the butchering day as a holiday when relatives get together, work hard, and savor each other's company. The family of Byard and Nellie Early, for example, gathers each year around Thanksgiving Day to butcher two hogs. Three generations assemble at the Earlys' home, introducing grandchildren to traditions observed in the family for years. Such days are not unusual in the valley, and for some the preservation of knowledge of the tradition is an important factor in the decision to continue butchering, as Janet Showalter, the mother of a seven-year-old and a three-year-old, noted in 1993: "[We] want our children to be exposed to it."

Naturally, butchering day is also important for the food it provides for the upcoming year, as Rosetta Harris remembered in 1976: "It was a long day. It was a hard day, but we had the pleasure of eating ponhoss and pudding with our breakfast hominy on cold winter mornings. We had fat meat to cook with the string beans next summer. We accepted fried ham with our eggs for breakfast and boiled ham for Sunday dinners as orthodox farm fare."

As this testimony demonstrates, pork is an essential part of much of the traditional valley diet. The region is renowned for its country ham, and individual sections of each county boast of their own well-known pork curers. From the time of subsistence farming in the valley, farmers have

Three generations of Byard and Nellie Early's family butchering hogs, 1993.

known how to cure their meat to not only preserve it but to also add flavor. In the nineteenth century Andrew Hess noted the following recipe for "salting" a thousand pounds of pork:

10 qts. salt
3 lbs. brown sugar
1 lbs. black pepper
2 oz. cayenne pepper

Mix all together

1 lbs. salt nitre
dissolved in 1 qt. of water
Mix with the above
Rub well on meat, rind and all

Another turn-of-the-century recipe, scrawled on the back of an envelope, calls for

4 lbs. salt
4 oz. brown sugar
4 oz. salt peter
for 100 lbs. meat

Continuing the tradition of meat preservation, contemporary meat curers tend to guard their recipes, believing that their special blends produce superior flavor.

Of course, recipes for preparing pork dishes also abound, and like the curing recipes, each one is slightly different, producing the cook's preferred taste. One of the most traditional meals produced from pork, known in the valley as ham pot pie, offers a good example of the variation caused by oral tradition and individual taste. The first recipe here is from Esther H. Shank, and the second was taken from the pages of my mother's cookbook.

Old-Fashioned Ham Pot Pie
(Use a mixture of ham broth and water to make a rich liquid. Ham broth is often salty, so use an amount that gives a good rich flavor that isn't too strong.)
4 cups broth and water   Heat to boiling
1 cup chopped cooked ham
3 medium potatoes, diced

Pot Pie Dough
1 large egg yolk, slightly beaten   Mix
1/8 tsp. salt
3 tbsp. water
approximately 2/3 cup flour

Add to make a stiff dough. Knead several times and roll out as thin as possible on floured surface. Cut into 1-inch squares. Drop into rapidly boiling broth. Cover and simmer 20 minutes.
Minced parsley to garnish   Sprinkle over top if desired.

Ham Pot Pie
2 cups flour   Mix together
$^1\!/_4$ tsp. salt
2 tbsp. shortening
Add $^1\!/_4$ cup water till dough sticks together.
Roll out as for pie dough—thin.
4 cups ham broth
Have broth come to boil. Add potatoes and dough. Add parsley and celery seed if desired.
Cook 15 minutes (on low) with lid on. Do not lift lid while cooking.
Better if you have some pieces of ham in the broth.

Of course, most cooks who know what they are doing add ingredients to satisfy their own tastes, and recipes become irrelevant.

Demonstrating the significance of this dish to Shenandoah Valley foodways, ham pot pie is frequently the main course at fund-raising dinners. Usually in the fall, churches, volunteer fire departments, and other civic organizations offer all-you-can-eat ham pot pie dinners to raise money for community activities. The menus often also include corn bread, white beans cooked in ham broth, cole slaw, and a dessert of gingerbread, all traditional foods in their own right. The large number of these events each year demonstrates the importance of this meal to the valley diet. Historically, too, ham pot pie has been a tasty, economical dish for serving large numbers of people. Writing in 1833, Samuel Kercheval recalled, "The standard dinner dish for every log-rolling, house-raising and harvest-day was a pot-pie." Community events, even in the early nineteenth century, involved a form of this folk food.

Fund-raising foods strongly reflect the community where they are consumed. Some regions prepare turtle soup, and others have clam bakes; in the Shenandoah Valley, where poultry is the chief industry, turkeys and chickens make the list alongside ham pot pie as important fund-raising foods. Barbecued chicken can be found for sale in public parking lots on almost any Saturday in the upper valley. Prepared early in the morning, chicken halves are wrapped in foil and sold while still warm, making them a good choice for a tasty lunch. Less frequent but just as successful are turkey, ham, and oyster dinners. Like the pot pie dinners, these events offer all you can eat of these dishes along with sauerkraut, cole slaw, and other vegetables usually prepared by members of the sponsoring group.

* * * * * * * * * *
NEED A BANQUET SERVED ?
RESERVE USE OF OUR PAVILION OR HALL
BY CALLING 434-3955
* * * * * * * * * *
Mt. Crawford Day - September 12, 1998
Yard Sale in Morning
Gospel Music in Afternoon
Ham Pot Pie - Applebutter
Turkey, Ham & Oyster Supper - Saturday, October 17, 1998

* * * * * * * * * *

Thank you for helping the
Mt. Crawford Ruritans accomplish
so much during the year.

Fund-raising advertisement, 1998.

The combination of the three main meats suggests the local importance of pork and poultry and demonstrates a taste for the exotic as well. As far back as the late nineteenth century oysters were a delicacy to be enjoyed as a festive food in the region. This combination of the common and the festive makes for a meal that many find difficult to turn down.

Many other food traditions exist in the Shenandoah Valley as families prepare the vegetables and fruits they raise in gardens or orchards or use the meat from animals they tended throughout the year. Fruit preserves, canned beans, horseradish, potato chips, and sausage are a few of the rewards of a hard season's work. Holiday foodways are also maintained in the region; many believe that pork and sauerkraut must be eaten on New Year's Day to ensure prosperity for the coming year, while others insist that black-eyed peas will guarantee good luck. Another traditional food that often serves as a money raiser is apple butter. As discussed earlier, apples have long been an important crop in the valley, and people enjoy buying the delicious apple spread that they know has been made the old-fashioned way—boiled in kettles—to get the proper flavor. The significance of these foodways to the Shenandoah Valley suggests that food preparation is one of the region's strongest traditions. As long as hogs are raised and butchered and apples are grown, valley residents will undoubtedly eat meals whose recipes are centuries old.

A study of folklife in the Shenandoah Valley paints a portrait of the past, but it is a portrait with contemporary faces. Much of the culture of the region's earliest European settlers has disappeared; however, their influence on late-twentieth-century valley culture is unmistakable. Agriculture remains the most important enterprise in the region, a reflection of subsistence farming in the eighteenth century, and although the techniques have changed, the land remains, and many families continue to work the same farms that their ancestors did, now literally feeding the world instead of just their relations.

Religion, too, offers glimpses of past traditions. Old Order Mennonites, shunning many of the unnecessary advances of modern society, travel the roads of Rockingham County in horse-drawn buggies, demonstrating that traditions can be maintained in the face of an encroaching culture of convenience. Mennonite values remain unchanged by time. Members of other churches also cling to methods of worship that while deemed old-fashioned by many hold deep meanings for those who attend the services. Again, these convictions carry over to secular aspects of life and encourage the maintenance of other traditional practices.

Many crafts of the past are carried on in the valley today, embroidering the present with images from more than two hundred years ago. Quilters gather at churches or in their homes, re-creating beautiful patterns that have been passed through generations at similar parties. Today, however, material is frequently purchased at stores, providing the artist with a more varied pallet than her ancestors, who often used available scraps and bits of used—but not worn out—clothing. The methods and patterns of the past endure with the flair of a modern eye. Often using centuries-old looms, rug weavers too employ ancient methods to produce usable, attractive floor coverings, carrying on family traditions and using designs as well as knowledge from the past. These rag rugs, truly valley folk art, illustrate the practical feature of all traditional art.

As the plight of the white oak basket-making tradition suggests, however, folklife often struggles to exist under the stressful conditions of modern society. The valley's growing population has contributed to the lack of available trees for these craftspeople as prime lands are appropriated to meet the expanding need for housing and services. Air pollution, also increasing with the population, blights the forest and reduces the chances for basket makers to find suitable materials. Cities have also begun to encroach on farmland, usurping land that has been farmed for centuries. Where dairy cattle once grazed, children now play in the backyards of suburban housing developments. As the landscape becomes saturated with new houses, architectural vestiges of the past are disappearing. Old houses reflecting the heritage of their builders are removed, and barns are allowed to fall, reminders of the gradual passing of traditional farming methods and large family farms.

The valley's population growth has also introduced a new mixture of folklife, replacing, in some cases, the old ways with new ones. Belsnickeling, for instance, no longer takes place. As transportation advances made commuting to and from work easier, residents could travel further from home, leading to an expansion of village neighborhoods and a decrease in visiting in the local community. No longer friendly with all their neighbors, people found the prospect of inviting masked strangers into their homes less appealing. These older traditions are being replaced, however, with others that are new to the valley, as recent arrivals to the region maintain their own traditional forms of music, food, and art.

Folklife exists in the Shenandoah Valley, bearing the marks of these recent changes as well as those from earlier periods. Like the furniture makers of the late nineteenth century who altered their designs to meet national tastes, some aspects of traditions are often retained in different forms that more clearly meet the needs of the culture currently practicing them. As the twentieth century turns into the twenty-first, the Shenandoah Valley uniquely presents pictures of life from the past two centuries and promises to continue to engender folklife, presenting a blending of the old and the new.

The following report, written at an undetermined time in the 1960s, is indicative of those produced by Elmer L. Smith and John G. Stewart when the authors were diligently interviewing Shenandoah Valley residents about the traditions that they practiced and remembered from times past. Smith, a professor of sociology, and Stewart, a professor of language, both at Madison College in Harrisonburg, Virginia, collaborated on numerous interviews and writing projects culminating in the book *Pennsylvania Germans of the Shenandoah Valley*, which they coauthored with M. Ellsworth Kyger, a professor at Bridgewater College in Bridgewater, Virginia. Smith and Stewart amassed a large library of recordings and photographs and produced many articles and booklets. Their work was the first of its kind in the valley and set the stage for further work in the field. Today, nearly forty years later, their fieldwork is even more important: many informants have died, and their knowledge of the traditions has been saved only by Smith and Stewart's work.

This brief, unpublished piece about the herb commonly known as masterwort is representative of the two folklorists' method of working—they discovered a tradition, superstition, or custom, found out what they could from informants, and then searched for the cultural antecedents in the European homeland of the practitioners' ancestors. Still informative, the work stands as an example of fieldwork and scholarship at an early stage of Shenandoah Valley folklife studies.

The Master Root—The Master of All Evil

Among the many folk medicine plants used by the Pennsylvania German settlers of the Shenandoah Valley and adjacent areas of West Virginia, the master root, mester warsel, takes a unique position. Several informants in Pendleton County, West Virginia, have stated that it is "the master of all evil," a cure against everything, even though its use today is somewhat limited. The writers have found that the superstitious flavor surrounding the name of the plant is based on old belief.

The master root, also called astrenze or strenze, (peucedanum ostruthium, imperatoria ostruthium) is an umbelliferous plant with coarse, ternate leaves. The stem is small and the blooms white with a light touch of red. It looks somewhat like dill. When eaten, the taste is bitter and unpleasant. Another characteristic is the strong aromatic flavor.

Dark places in mountainous regions are its primary locations, but it can be planted in home gardens as a perennial. December is the most favorable planting time. It should be transplanted in May so that blooms appear in late summer.

The characteristics of the plant, being strongly aromatic and tasting bitter, are reasons for the superstitions connected with its use. The strange look of the plants, blooms outside the seasons, biological peculiarities, and poisonous effects are other qualities of plants that play a part in superstition.

Several informants used the plant for various purposes. The writers have seen the master root in one garden and have had locations of gardens pointed out where the plant was grown in former years. "Grandfather and Grandmother planted it. That was over a hundred years ago." "My Aunt Mary had it in her garden together with narrow sage and old men's beard. It all died when the old folks passed away. We all called it 'master of all evil.' " "Old Amy Puffenbarger and Sue Simmons raised it here. They made me a tea with it." One informant stated that master root was fed to the "broots" (cattle). It was cut into pieces and given to the cattle to eat. "There was nothing wrong with the cattle but we gave it to keep them from getting 'something.' " Another informant also said that cattle were fed with it but that it was much better as a cure for fever: "It used to be raised by two neighbors and my mother always made tea with it for me when I had fever. The fever was broken." An elderly man remembered that it was fed to cattle so that they would not give bloody milk. The belief that the master root died when the owners of the garden died was expressed by several informants. "We used it secretly, just the root." "Cory Pennybaker raised master root. He put it under his hunting coat so that it would stop the spell on dogs." "It was against any kind of sickness. We used it against childbed fever."

The belief that the master root was the master of all evil must have been an oral tradition transmitted through generations of people of Germanic background. It is reported that the plant was very popular in central Europe as a means of protection from various evils.

In the 1670 edition of Bernard Verzascha's *Neu Vollkommenes Krauterbuch,* which was in the possession of Baron von Stiegel, it is stated that the master root is "excellent against all poison, especially pestilence." It also helps in case of bad mouth odor, stomach trouble, sexual impotence in men and women, bladder trouble, and afterbirth difficulties. The author characterizes the plant as *hizig* with a strong odor and a bitter taste—"it burns in the mouth like pepper." When planted, a distance of "one shoe" should be observed between plants. The smaller *bergmeisterwuz* is more juicy.

Various other sources should also contribute to the explanation of the belief that the plant was the master of all evil. In Bohemia and Silesia a cow that did not give milk was fed garlic, bread, salt, and master root. In several locations in Central Europe the plant was blessed in church. Cattle and horses were fed with the plant to keep witches away from them. As a protection against abscesses and other diseases of pigs, a mixture of hog grease, egg yolk, and master root was used. Against headaches and tooth-aches, three pipes full mixture of dried master root should be smoked. In case of abscessed wounds caused by arrows or bullets, master root, placed on the open wound, was supposed to be a means of counteracting the im-plements of war. If a person has consumption, seven pieces of master root should be given him. The root must be pulled out of the ground on Holy Friday or any Friday when there is a full moon. Add seven pieces of a coffin in which a pregnant woman was buried.

Widespread use of the root as an amulet has also been reported. Against sore eyes, red silk string should be worn around the neck with seven to nine master roots tied to it. In the Canton Aargau in Switzerland, wasps were kept away by a mixture of bread, dust, and master root. These ingredi-ents were put together and tied on a barn door. As a permanent protection against witches, small pieces of blessed resin, bark, and master root were buried under the threshold of a barn. Blessed candles, bread, and master root were also used for this purpose.

Against coughing and head colds, one should dig master root at the time of increase of the moon. The root is to be tied on the back of the afflicted person. After use, throw the root into a river. Tied on thumbs and toes, it was a remedy against epilepsy.

The old belief that the plant was one of the cures for a variety of diseases has undergone many changes throughout the years. Superstition still sur-rounds the name of the master root. The limited use made of the plant today, however, is only one example of a combination of folk and sympa-thetic medicine with a touch of brauche. Those informants who talked to the writers simply follow old established practices once prevalent among their own people.

Settlement

The earliest history of the Shenandoah Valley is Samuel Kercheval's *A History of the Valley of Virginia,* first published in 1833 and now in its fourth edition. While many of Kercheval's ideas are now disputed, this book remains fascinating for anyone interested in stories about life in the valley at the turn of the nineteenth century. Furthermore, many histories of Shenandoah Valley counties have been written over the years, offering stories of settlement and often the authors' views of the development of a distinctive culture in the region. In addition to the following titles, other books are listed in the bibliography. John W. Wayland's *The German Element of the Shenandoah Valley, A History of Rockingham County Virginia,* and *A History of Shenandoah County Virginia* were all originally published in the first quarter of the twentieth century and provide good accounts of their topics. J. E. Norris's *History of the Lower Shenandoah Valley,* although published in 1890, offers a detailed history of Frederick, Berkeley, Jefferson, and Clarke Counties and ends with the obligatory late-nineteenth-century account of the region's significance in the Civil War. Similarly, Thomas Gold's *Clarke County, Virginia, and Its Connection with the War between the States* devotes more than two-thirds of its pages to the war. Harry M. Strickler published *A Short History of Page County, Virginia* in 1952, and it remains the only history of that county. J. Lewis Peyton's *History of Augusta County, Virginia* appeared in 1882 and provides many interesting accounts that only a nineteenth-century writer could have captured. A more recent history is Richard K. MacMaster's *Augusta County History, 1865–1950.* The early history of Frederick County is recounted in *Shenandoah Valley Pioneers and Their Descendants: A History of Frederick County, Virginia,* which T. K. Cartmell published in 1909. Although not a county history itself, Gordon W. Miller's *Rockingham: An Annotated Bibliography of a Virginia County* is an indispensable resource for studying the history of Rockingham County and by extension the entire region.

Along with Wayland's study of the Germans in the valley, there are other important cultural studies; foremost among books on the region's folklife is *The Pennsylvania Germans of the Shenandoah Valley*. Written by Elmer Lewis Smith, John G. Stewart, and M. Ellsworth Kyger and published in 1964, this book is based on years of research and fieldwork and stands as the first book-length study of traditional life in the Shenandoah Valley. The three authors were pioneers in the study of valley traditions and their antecedents.

Parke Rouse Jr.'s *The Great Wagon Road: From Philadelphia to the South* offers a readable look at the history of the entire valley of Virginia, including those sections south of the Shenandoah Valley. A more localized—and entertaining—account is *Life along Holman's Creek, Shenandoah County, Virginia*, by Joseph Floyd Wine. Originally published in 1912, Lyman Chalkley's three-volume *Chronicles of the Scotch-Irish Settlement in Virginia* offers a wealth of information on the Scots-Irish as well as other settlers in the valley.

All of the material on Native Americans presented in chapter 1 comes from Darwin Lambert's *The Undying Past of Shenandoah National Park*. Along with his review of Native American life in the region, he provides a concise history of the land in and around the national park. Klaus Wust's *The Virginia Germans* is the most comprehensive study of that group in the state, and it offers in-depth coverage of ethnic life in the Shenandoah Valley. One of the most useful books on the early valley is Robert D. Mitchell's *Commercialism on the Frontier: Perspectives on the Early Shenandoah Valley*. Although this work focuses on the region's economic history, the study has much to offer students of cultural and social history. Along with Mitchell's work, J. Susanne Simmons's master's thesis, "They Too Were Here: African-Americans in Augusta County and Staunton, Virginia, 1745–1865," and Dorothy A. Boyd-Rush's *Registry of Free Blacks, Rockingham County, Virginia, 1807–1859* provide insight into the history of Africans and African Americans in the valley. Much research remains to be done on this topic, however.

Performance

Very little has been written about traditional music in the Shenandoah Valley. The exhibition "Fine-Tuned Folks: The Culture of String Music in the Shenandoah Valley" and its gallery guide written by Kevin Harter are the sole contributions toward bringing string-band research in the Shenandoah Valley to the public. Held at the Shenandoah Valley Folk Art and Heritage Center in Dayton, Virginia, in 1996, the exhibit explored the importance of community to the sound of contemporary string music in the valley. The guide, while necessarily brief, is one of the few pieces of scholarly writing on this important tradition. The quotations from Ellsworth Kyger are from an interview conducted by Harter. Raymond Bynaker's statements are from Harter's unpublished manuscript, "Raymond's Picking Parlor and the Nurturance of a Musical Community."

Field interviews that I conducted in 1990 as a part of a folk-arts survey of the Shenandoah Valley for the Virginia Folklife Program have been integral to my understanding of the nature of traditional music in the valley. Along with A. O. Knicely and Dalton Brill, who are quoted in this chapter, I also talked with Wilbur Terry, Bob Driver, Lester Ryman, and Sam Glynn. Together with my own experience as a musician, these conversations have influenced my thinking on how traditional string music in the valley is perpetuated.

The history of bluegrass music throughout the world can be found in Neil Rosenberg, *Bluegrass: A History,* while Robert Cantwell's *Bluegrass Breakdown* offers an excellent analysis of that musical genre. Manuel Peña's "The Texas-Mexican Conjunto" provides a concise and informative background to a style of ethnic music that is becoming more prevalent in the valley.

Little, too, has been written regarding the ballad tradition in the Shenandoah Valley. Arthur Kyle Davis Jr.'s *Ballads of Virginia* is the sole collection of this musical genre that covers all of Virginia. Although this work offers an interesting introduction to balladry, it fails to cover valley traditions in any detail. The lyrics of "Lady Marget" appear on pp. 224–25 of Davis's work. The lyrics of "The Butcher Boy" are from Kelly Harrell's 1925 recording for the Victor Record Company [Victor 20242]. Born in 1889, Harrell hailed from Wythe County, Virginia, south of the Shenandoah Valley; however, his version would have been similar to that of valley singers. Harrell's recording can be found on *Virginia Traditions: Ballads from British Tradition.*

Wust treats the music of Germans in the valley in *The Virginia Germans,* looking primarily at religious choral music and the growth of singing schools. He also offers a concise history of the Funk family from Mountain Valley, later Singers Glen, and the impact of their publication, *The Harmonia Sacra,* on gospel music in the valley and beyond. Kip Lornell's chapter on Anglo-American sacred folk music in his *Introducing American Folk Music* provides a good introduction to gospel-music traditions in the valley, while Charles K. Wolfe's entry, "Gospel Music, White," in Charles Reagan Wilson and William Ferris's *Encyclopedia of Southern Culture* and John Minton's piece, "Shape-Note Singing," in Jan Harold Brunvand's *American Folklore: An Encyclopedia* furnish good overviews of the topic.

A number of publications provide information on belsnickeling, kriskringling, and shanghaiing. Smith, Stewart, and Kyger treat the subject in their *Pennsylvania Germans of the Shenandoah Valley,* and Gerald Milnes looks at the tradition in neighboring West Virginia in "Old Christmas and Belsnickles: Our Early Holiday Traditions." Stewart also explores the origins specifically of shanghaiing in his essay "Shanghaiing in the Valley of Virginia." Elmer Smith's collections of tapes are housed in the Blue Ridge Heritage Archives at Ferrum College in Ferrum, Virginia. My interviews with Ryman, Brill, Ruby Wagner, Mary Hulvey, and Clara Jean Comer reveal much about traditions as they were practiced in the valley from the 1930s through the 1960s. The information regarding the unfortunate belsnickels in Bridgewater is found in Roger E. Sappington's *The Brethren in Bridgewater: First Hundred Years.* Jack Santino discusses the Celtic holiday Samhain in the introduction to *Halloween and Other Festivals of Death and Life,* while Henry Glassie examines an Irish Christmas tradition that includes costumed performers in *All Silver and No Brass: An Irish Christmas Mumming.*

There are many scholarly texts on folk narrative traditions. Dan Ben-Amos's definition is found in *Folklore, Cultural Performances, and Popular Entertainments,* edited by Richard Bauman. Another useful introduction is the section on oral folklore in Brunvand, *The Study of American Folklore.* The story of the McChesney ghost is widely known; I have quoted the version found in Joseph A. Waddell's *Annals of Augusta County, Virginia: From 1726–1871* since he spoke with a witness to these events. John L. Heatwole's collection, *Shenandoah Voices: Folklore, Legends, and Traditions of the Valley,* offers a variety of narratives from throughout the Shenandoah Valley; Wine's *Tales from Shenandoah* is also a small collection of stories, both true and legendary, from the region. Galen Miller Sr. recounted his tales of the early Rockingham County Baseball League to Richard Gaughran and me in 1995.

Unfortunately, no large collection of Shenandoah Valley folk narratives has been produced, and Thomas Barden's edition, *Virginia Legends,* contains no stories from the region. Along with Barden's work, there are two notable books that explore narratives in the eastern United States: *Jack in Two Worlds: Contemporary North American Tales and Their Tellers,* edited by William Bernard McCarthy, and *Storytellers: Folktales and Legends from the South,* edited by John A. Burrison. Both works look at contemporary traditions.

Social Institutions

RELIGION

The definition of religious folklore quoted at the beginning of the chapter is from Larry Danielson's chapter in Elliott Oring's *Folk Groups and Folklore Genres: An Introduction*. Don Yoder discusses folk religion in a number of publications, including "Toward a Definition of Folk Religion" and "Official Religion versus Folk Religion." William Clements's theories appear in his "The American Folk Church in Northeast Arkansas." Another short, general introduction to the topic, written by Jennifer E. Livesay and Kenneth D. Pimple, appears under the heading "Religion, Folk" in Brunvand's *American Folklore: An Encyclopedia*.

The discussion of the Fellowship Independent Baptist Church comes entirely from the comprehensive work of Jeff Todd Titon. The information in this chapter is found in *Powerhouse for God: Speech, Chant, and Song in an Appalachian Baptist Church*, particularly chapter 3. Titon has also produced, along with Tom Rankin and Barry Dornfeld, a film by the same title as well as a sound recording of sermons, prayers, and songs from the church. They are essential material for anyone seeking to understand Baptist traditions in the Appalachian Mountains and Shenandoah Valley.

There is much literature on the Mennonite Church in America; however, I have found two works particularly helpful in understanding the varieties of the Mennonite experience. Calvin Redekop's *Mennonite Society* is undoubtedly the most scholarly study of the Mennonite Church to date, exploring the origins of the movement as well as focusing on contemporary Mennonites in North America, and Stephen Scott's *An Introduction to Old Order and Conservative Mennonite Groups* serves as an excellent introduction for those seeking to learn about this group on a more general level. Theron F. Schlabach provides an in-depth history of Mennonite life during the 1800s in *Peace, Faith, Nation: Mennonites and Amish in Nineteenth-Century America*. The quotations by Albert Keim and Lewis Martin are found in Joan Vannorsdall Schroeder's brief but insightful article, "Virginia's Rockingham County Mennonites: Tender Conscience and Acts of Violence." Dated but nevertheless useful is Harry Anthony Brunk's two-volume *History of Mennonites in Virginia*.

The story of the Dunkers, or Church of the Brethren, is most completely and expertly told by Carl F. Bowman in *Brethren Society: The Cultural Transformation of a "Peculiar People,"* with the description of the Brethren baptism on pp. 51–53. Other useful and informative essays appear in *Brethren in Transition: Twentieth Century Directions and Dilemmas*, edited by Emmert F. Bittinger. Nancy Kettering Frye looks at the designs of meetinghouses in "The Meetinghouse Connection: Plain Living in the Gilded Age." Terry Barkley's *One Who Served: Brethren Elder Charles Nesselrodt of Shenandoah County, Virginia* is a useful and interesting biography of an early-twentieth-century Brethren minister.

FOLK MEDICINE AND BELIEFS

James W. Kirkland provides an authoritative introduction to folk medicine in his entry in Brunvand's *American Folklore: An Encyclopedia*. Similarly, Yoder's in-depth chapter on the topic in Richard Dorson's *Folklore and Folklife* offers a general study for gaining an understanding of the topic and how folklorists have studied it.

All of the material quoted from nineteenth-century personal books is taken from Stewart's personal collection. Additional information, including interviews and a discussion of brauche, can be found in Smith, Stewart, and Kyger's *Pennsylvania Germans of the Shenandoah Valley*. Benjamin Funk's reminiscences of John Kline are recorded in *Life and Labors of Elder John Kline, the Martyr Missionary*. Harter's interviews with ginseng growers are collected in an unpublished paper, " 'Hey, I Got Ginseng Planted': Ginseng Growers in Rockingham County, Virginia."

FAIRS AND FESTIVALS

Concise introductions to the role of fairs and festivals in traditional life are found under those headings in Brunvand's *American Folklife: An Encyclopedia*. The definition of fairs used in the text is from Joyce Ice's entry in that book. Leslie Prosterman's *Ordinary Life, Festival Days: Aesthetics in the Midwestern County Fair*, while focusing on another region, offers an excellent study of county fairs and the important traditions imbedded within their contests and events. Orra Langhorne's report on the Harrisonburg Spring Fair is included in Charles E. Wynes's edition of her writing, *Southern Sketches from Virginia, 1881–1901*. Information on the early days of the Shenandoah Apple Blossom Festival can be found in the *Winchester Evening Star* from April 1924, while a history of the event's founding is included in Katherine Glass Greene, Philip Williams, and W. W. Glass's "Winchester, Frederick County, and the Shenandoah Apple Blossom Festival." Turkey Festival information is recorded mostly in the souvenir guides for 1939 and 1940.

MATERIAL CULTURE

There are many sources of information on the broad topic of the Shenandoah Valley's material folk culture, and most sources follow a definition of traditional objects similar to John Michael Vlach's insightful description of folk things in "The Concept of Community and Folklife Study." *Folk and Decorative Art of the Shenandoah Valley*, compiled by the Shenandoah Valley Folklore Society, provides a useful and copiously illustrated introduction to traditional crafts and arts of the region, and Glassie's work, *Pattern in the Material Folk Culture of the Eastern United States*, although more than thirty years old, still offers one of the best introductions to the subject of traditional material culture, including discussions of objects from the Shenandoah Valley. Smith, Stewart, and Kyger's *Pennsylvania Germans of the Shenandoah Valley* contains chapters on fraktur, crafts, printing, and gravestones and cemeteries. The "jackleg" blacksmith from Augusta County is John Yowell.

Individual genres of material culture require specific studies, and I have drawn on a number of such works in this chapter. A. H. Rice and John Baer Stoudt first recorded the history of ceramic production in the lower valley in their 1929 work, *The Shenandoah Pottery*, and H. E. Comstock furthered the study with his thorough examination, *The Pottery of the Shenandoah Valley Region*. My dissertation, " 'The Importance of Making Progress': The Potteries of Emanuel Suter, 1851–1897," considers the influence of region and technology on one traditional valley potter.

Studies of cabinetmakers in the valley include Wallace B. Gusler, "The Arts of Shenandoah County, Virginia 1770–1825," and Nina Norem Maurer's master's thesis, "Limits of Conservatism: Cabinetmaker Adam Kersh." My catalog for the 1996 exhibition "Tradition and Fashion: Cabinetmaking in the Upper Shenandoah Valley, 1850–1900" offers discussions of the Theis brothers and three other furniture makers of the period—Alexander Coffman, Adam Kersh, and Daniel Suter.

Nancy J. Martin-Perdue's essay, "On Eaton's Trail: A Genealogical Study of Virginia Basket Makers," provides much of the history of the Nicholson family, which continues to make baskets in the valley. While not specific to the Shenandoah Valley, *Appalachian White Oak Basketmaking: Handing down the Basket*, by Rachel Nash Law and Cynthia W. Taylor, places the valley's tradition within the context of white oak basket making throughout the Appalachian region. Interviews that I conducted for the Virginia Folklife Program in 1990 and 1992 with basket makers Bill and James Cook, Gregory and Ernest Nicholas, John Nichols, Elmer Price Sr., Max Price, and Philip and Cathy Cook Sheetz offered much insight into the tradition and process of basket making as well as into the plight of the craft. My essays "White Oak Basketmaking's Uncertain Future" and "Appreciating the Tree" address some of the important issues facing these traditional craftspeople.

Glassie's lyrical observations on folk architecture can be found in "Artifact and Culture, Architecture and Society," and his remarks on German and Irish house types in *Pattern in the Material Folk Culture of the Eastern United States* form the basis of the discussion of the valley's early ethnic housing. Edward A. Chappell provides the most in-depth analysis of German housing in "Cultural Change in the Shenandoah Valley: Northern Augusta County Houses before 1861" and "Acculturation in the Shenandoah Valley: Rhenish Houses of the Massanutten Settlement." Both Glassie and Chappell contribute concise entries on ethnic housing in the valley to Dell Upton's *America's Architectural Roots: Ethnic Groups That Built America*. Ann McCleary discusses architectural changes in the nineteenth-century valley in "Domesticity and the Farm Woman: A Case Study of Women in Augusta County, Virginia, 1850–1940."

Two studies examine the significance of the forebay bank barn in the greater Pennsylvania region. Joseph W. Glass's *The Pennsylvania Culture Region: A View from the Barn* offers a cultural geographer's opinion of how the structures communicate culture. Robert F. Ensminger, also a geographer, traces the origins of the barn type and demonstrates how the movement of the barn across the United States reflects a movement of cultural ideas as well as common sense. His findings appear in *The Pennsylvania Barn: Its Origin, Evolution, and Distribution in North America*. The description of the barn raising in Rockingham County appears in the July 3, 1937, edition of the *Harrisonburg Daily News Record*.

Charles Camp's *American Foodways: What, When, Why, and How We Eat in America* is a concise but important study of food in American culture, and it forms the basis of my examination of food culture in the Shenandoah Valley. Other sources of information include a December 22, 1993, *Harrisonburg Daily News Record* interview with Janet and Galen Showalter and a butchering day that I spent with Byard and Nellie Early's family in 1994. Rosetta Harris's recollections of butchering and the year-round importance of pork to the valley diet can be found on pp. 83–84 of Nancy B. Hess's *The Heartland: Rockingham County*. Andrew Hess's recipe for salting pork is written in his record book, and the turn-of-the-century envelope is in the collection of the Harrisonburg-Rockingham Historical Society. Esther Shank's recipe for ham pot pie is included in her *Mennonite Country-Style Recipes and Kitchen Secrets*. Kercheval's memory of pot pie appears on p. 247 of his history.

Abrahams, Roger D. *Singing the Master: The Emergence of African-American Culture in the Plantation South.* New York: Penguin Books, 1992.

Barden, Thomas E., ed. *Virginia Folk Legends.* Charlottesville: University Press of Virginia, 1991.

Barkley, Terry. *One Who Served: Brethren Elder Charles Nesselrodt of Shenandoah County, Virginia.* Bridgewater, Va.: privately published, 1996.

Bauman, Richard, ed. *Folklore, Cultural Performances, and Popular Entertainments: A Communications-Centered Handbook.* New York: Oxford University Press, 1992.

Bittinger, Emmert F. *Brethren in Transition: Twentieth Century Directions and Dilemmas.* Camden, Maine: Penobscot Press, 1992.

Bolgiano, Chris. *The Appalachian Forest: A Search for Roots and Renewal.* Mechanicsburg, Pa.: Stackpole Books, 1998.

Bowman, Carl F. *Brethren Society: The Cultural Transformation of a "Peculiar People."* Baltimore: Johns Hopkins University Press, 1995.

Boyd-Rush, Dorothy A. *Registry of Free Blacks, Rockingham County, Virginia, 1807–1859.* Bowie, Md.: Heritage Books, 1992.

Branch, Michael P., and Daniel J. Philippon, eds. *The Height of Our Mountains: Nature Writing from Virginia's Blue Ridge Mountains and Shenandoah Valley.* Baltimore: Johns Hopkins University Press, 1998.

Brown, Amy Walker. "Buried Folklore in the Shenandoah Valley." Unpublished paper, Special Collections, James Madison University, 1993.

Brown, Katherine L. *Traditional Christmas Customs.* Staunton, Va.: American Frontier Culture Foundation, 1997.

Brown, Stuart E. *Clarke County: A Brief History.* White Post, Va.: Clarke County Sesquicentennial Committee, 1986.

Brunk, Harry Anthony. *History of Mennonites in Virginia, 1727–1900.* Vol. 1. Harrisonburg, Va.: H. A. Brunk, 1959.

———. *History of Mennonites in Virginia, 1900–1960.* Vol. 2. Verona, Va.: McClure Printing, 1972.

Brunvand, Jan Harold, ed. *American Folklore: An Encyclopedia.* New York: Garland, 1996.

———. *The Study of American Folklore: An Introduction.* 3d ed. New York: Norton, 1986.

Burkholder, E. Daniel, Jr. *Carriage Makers of Rockingham County, Virginia, 1820–1997.* Dayton, Va.: privately published, 1997.

Burrison, John A., ed. *Storytellers: Folktales and Legends from the South*. Athens: University of Georgia Press, 1991.

Camp, Charles. *American Foodways: What, When, Why, and How We Eat in America*. Little Rock, Ark.: August House, 1989.

Cantwell, Robert. *Bluegrass Breakdown: The Making of the Old Southern Sound*. Urbana: University of Illinois Press, 1984.

Carr, Maria G. *My Recollections of Rocktown, Now Known as Harrisonburg*. 1959. Reprint, Harrisonburg, Va: Harrisonburg-Rockingham Historical Society, 1984.

Cartmell, T. K. *Shenandoah Valley Pioneers and Their Descendants: A History of Frederick County, Virginia*. Winchester, Va.: Eddy Press, 1909.

Chalkley, Lyman. *Chronicles of the Scotch-Irish Settlement in Virginia*. 1912–13. Reprint, Baltimore: Genealogical Publishing, 1965.

Chappell, Edward A. "Acculturation in the Shenandoah Valley: Rhenish Houses of the Massanutten Settlement." In *Common Places: Readings in American Vernacular Architecture*, ed. Dell Upton and John Michael Vlach, 27–57. Athens: University of Georgia Press, 1986.

———. "Cultural Change in the Shenandoah Valley: Northern Augusta County Houses before 1861." Master's thesis, University of Virginia, 1977.

Clements, William M. "The American Folk Church in Northeast Arkansas." *Journal of the Folklore Institute* 15 (1978): 161–80.

Comstock, H. E. *The Pottery of the Shenandoah Valley Region*. Winston-Salem, N.C.: Museum of Early Southern Decorative Arts, 1994.

Davis, Arthur Kyle, Jr., ed. *Traditional Ballads of Virginia*. 1929. Reprint, Charlottesville: University Press of Virginia, 1969.

Dickinson, Josiah Look. *The Fairfax Proprietary: The Northern Neck, the Fairfax Manors, and Beginnings of Warren County in Virginia*. Front Royal, Va.: Warren Press, 1959.

Dorson, Richard, ed. *Folklore and Folklife: An Introduction*. Chicago: University of Chicago Press, 1972.

Downs, Janet Baugher, and Earl J. Downs. *Mills of Rockingham County*. Vol. 1. Dayton, Va.: Harrisonburg-Rockingham Historical Society, 1997.

———. *Mills of Rockingham County*. Vol. 2. Dayton, Va.: Harrisonburg-Rockingham Historical Society, 1998.

Ensminger, Robert F. *The Pennsylvania Barn: Its Origin, Evolution, and Distribution in North America*. Baltimore: Johns Hopkins University Press, 1992.

Fogleman, Aaron Spencer. *Hopeful Journeys: German Immigration, Settlement, and Political Culture in Colonial America, 1717–1775*. Philadelphia: University of Pennsylvania Press, 1996.

Frye, Nancy Kettering. "The Meetinghouse Connection: Plain Living in the Gilded Age." *Pennsylvania Folklife* 41 (winter 1991–92): 50–82.

Funk, Benjamin. *Life and Labors of Elder John Kline, the Martyr Missionary.* Elgin, Ill.: Brethren Publishing House, 1900.

Funk, John, ed. *The Family Dyer, Being a Complete Guide for Colouring Every Variety of Shade, on Woolen, Cotton, Linen, and Silk Goods.* 1848. Reprint, Dayton, Va.: Harrisonburg-Rockingham Historical Society, 1998.

Gardner, William M. *Lost Arrowheads and Broken Pottery: Traces of Indians in the Shenandoah Valley.* Manassas, Va.: Thunderbird Publications, 1986.

Glass, Joseph W. *The Pennsylvania Culture Region: A View from the Barn.* Ann Arbor: UMI Research Press, 1986.

Glassie, Henry. *All Silver and No Brass: An Irish Christmas Mumming.* Philadelphia: University of Pennsylvania Press, 1983.

———. "Artifact and Culture, Architecture and Society." In *American Material Culture and Folklife: A Prologue and Dialogue,* ed. Simon J. Bronner, 47–62. Logan: Utah State University Press, 1992.

———. *Pattern in the Material Folk Culture of the Eastern United States.* Philadelphia: University of Pennsylvania Press, 1969.

———. "The Pennsylvania Barn in the South." *Pennsylvania Folklife* 15 (winter 1965–66): 8–19; (summer 1966): 12–25.

Gold, Thomas D. *History of Clarke County, Virginia, and Its Connection with the War between the States.* Berryville, Va.: n.p., 1914.

Greene, Katherine Glass, Philip Williams, and W. W. Glass. "Winchester, Frederick County, and the Shenandoah Apple Blossom Festival." *University of Virginia Record Extension Series* 15 (August 1930): 1–28.

Gusler, Wallace B. "The Arts of Shenandoah County, Virginia, 1770–1825." *Journal of Early Southern Decorative Arts* (November 1979): 6–35.

Hammond, Gene Paige. *Some Shenandoah Valley Mennonite Settlers: Where They Came from, Who They Were.* Strasburg, Va.: G.P. Hammond, 1992.

Harter, Kevin. "Fine-Tuned Folks: The Culture of String Music in the Shenandoah Valley." Gallery Guide for Exhibition at the Shenandoah Valley Folk Art and Heritage Center, Dayton, Va.: Harrisonburg-Rockingham Historical Society, 1997.

———. " 'Hey, I Got Ginseng Planted': Ginseng Growers in Rockingham County, Virginia." Unpublished paper, 1994.

Heatwole, John L. *Magic Cures and Incantations.* Bridgewater, Va.: privately published, 1997.

———. *Shenandoah Voices: Folklore, Legends, and Traditions of the Valley.* Berryville, Va.: Rockbridge Publishing, 1995.

———. *Superstitions.* Bridgewater, Va.: privately published, 1997.

————. *Witches and Witch Doctors.* Bridgewater, Va.: privately published, 1997.

Hess, Nancy B., ed. *The Heartland: Rockingham County.* Harrisonburg, Va.: Park View Press, 1976.

Hildebrand, John R., ed. *A Mennonite Journal, 1862–1865: A Father's Account of the Civil War in the Shenandoah Valley.* Shippensburg, Pa.: Burd Street Press, 1996.

Kaufman, Stanley A. *Heatwole and Suter Pottery.* Harrisonburg, Va.: Good Printers, 1978.

Kercheval, Samuel. *A History of the Valley of Virginia.* 4th ed. Harrisonburg, Va.: C. J. Carrier, 1994.

Kidney, Walter C., and James R. Morrison. *Winchester: Limestone, Sycamores, and Architecture.* Winchester, Va.: Preservation of Historic Winchester, 1977.

Kline, Agnes. *Stone Houses on Linville Creek and Their Communities.* 1971. Reprint, Dayton, Va.: Harrisonburg-Rockingham Historical Society, 1997.

Lambert, Darwin. *The Undying Past of Shenandoah National Park.* Boulder, Co.: Roberts Rinehart, 1989.

Langhorne, Orra. *Southern Sketches from Virginia, 1881–1901.* Ed. Charles E. Wynes. Charlottesville: University Press of Virginia, 1964.

Law, Rachel Nash, and Cynthia W. Taylor. *Appalachian White Oak Basketmaking: Handing down the Basket.* Knoxville: University of Tennessee Press, 1991.

Locke, Louis G. "Antique Furniture of the Shenandoah Valley." *Virginia Cavalcade* 24 (winter 1975): 108–15.

Lornell, Kip. *Introducing American Folk Music.* Madison, Wis.: Brown and Benchmark, 1993.

Lott, George. "Alexander Coffman, 1842–1920." *Chronicle of the Early American Industries Association* 48 (December 1995): 69–73.

MacMaster, Richard K. *Augusta County History, 1865–1950.* Staunton, Va.: Augusta County Historical Society, 1987.

Martin-Perdue, Nancy J. "On Eaton's Trail: A Genealogical Study of Virginia Basket Makers." In *Traditional Craftsmanship in America,* ed. Charles Camp, 79–101. Washington, D.C.: National Council for the Traditional Arts.

Maurer, Nina Norem. "Limits of Conservatism: Cabinetmaker Adam Kersh." Master's thesis, University of Delaware, 1992.

McCarthy, William Bernard, ed. *Jack in Two Worlds: Contemporary North American Tales and Their Tellers.* Chapel Hill: University of North Carolina Press, 1994.

McCleary, Ann. "Domesticity and the Farm Woman: A Case Study of

Women in Augusta County, Virginia, 1850–1940." *Perspectives in Vernacular Architecture* 1:25–30.

Mercer, Henry Chapman. "The Survival of the Mediaeval Art of Illuminative Writing among Pennsylvania Germans." In *Proceedings of the American Philosophical Society* 36 (December 1897): 424–33.

Miller, Gordon W. *Rockingham: An Annotated Bibliography of a Virginia County.* Harrisonburg, Va: Harrisonburg-Rockingham Historical Society, 1989.

Milnes, Gerald. "Old Christmas and Belsnickles: Our Early Holiday Traditions." *Goldenseal* 21 (winter 1995): 26–31.

Mitchell, Robert D. *Commercialism on the Frontier: Perspectives on the Early Shenandoah Valley.* Charlottesville: University Press of Virginia, 1977.

Norris, J. E., ed. *History of the Lower Shenandoah Valley Counties of Frederick, Berkeley, Jefferson, and Clarke.* Chicago: A. Warner, 1890.

Oring, Elliott, ed. *Folk Groups and Folklore Genres: An Introduction.* Logan: Utah State University Press, 1986.

Peacock, James L., and Ruel W. Tyson, Jr. *Pilgrims of Paradox: Calvinism and Experience among the Primitive Baptists of the Blue Ridge.* Washington, D.C.: Smithsonian Institution Press, 1989.

Peña, Manuel. "The Texas-Mexican Conjunto." In *1993 Festival of American Folklife,* 53–55. Washington, D.C.: Smithsonian Institution, 1993.

Peyton, J. Lewis. *History of Augusta County, Virginia.* 2d ed. Harrisonburg, Va.: C. J. Carrier, 1953.

Prosterman, Leslie. *Ordinary Life, Festival Days: Aesthetics in the Midwestern County Fair.* Washington, D.C.: Smithsonian Institution Press, 1995.

Redekop, Calvin. *Mennonite Society.* Baltimore: Johns Hopkins University Press, 1989.

Rice, A. H., and John Baer Stoudt. *The Shenandoah Pottery.* 1929. Reprint, Berryville, Va.: Virginia Book Company, 1974.

Rosenberg, Neil V. *Bluegrass: A History.* Urbana: University of Illinois Press, 1985.

———. *The Folksongs of Virginia: A Checklist of the WPA Holdings, Alderman Library, University of Virginia.* Charlottesville: University Press of Virginia, 1969.

Rouse, Parke, Jr. *The Great Wagon Road: From Philadelphia to the South.* Richmond, Va.: Dietz Press, 1995.

Santino, Jack, ed. *Halloween and Other Festivals of Death and Life.* Knoxville: University of Tennessee Press, 1994.

Sappington, Roger E. *The Brethren in Bridgewater: First Hundred Years.* Harrisonburg, Va.: Park View Press, 1978.

———. *The Brethren in Virginia: The History of the Church of the Brethren in Virginia.* Harrisonburg, Va.: Park View Press, 1973.

Schlabach, Theron F. *Peace, Faith, Nation: Mennonites and Amish in Nine-teenth-Century America.* Scottdale, Pa.: Herald Press, 1988.

Schroeder, Joan Vannorsdall. "Virginia's Rockingham County Mennon-ites: Tender Conscience and Acts of Violence." *Blue Ridge Country* (January–February 1992): 18–21.

Scott, Stephen. *An Introduction to Old Order and Conservative Mennonite Groups.* Intercourse, Pa.: Good Books, 1996.

Shank, Esther H. *Mennonite Country-Style Recipes and Kitchen Secrets.* Scott-dale, Pa.: Herald Press, 1987.

Shenandoah Valley Folklore Society. *Folk and Decorative Art of the Shenan-doah Valley.* Bridgewater, Va.: Good Printers, 1993.

Showalter, Mary Emma. *Mennonite Community Cookbook.* Scottdale, Pa.: Herald Press, 1950.

Simmons, J. Susanne. "They Too Were Here: African-Americans in Au-gusta County and Staunton, Virginia, 1745–1865." Master's thesis, James Madison University, 1994.

Smith, Dorothy Noble. *Recollections: The People of the Blue Ridge Remember.* Ed. James F. Gorman. Verona, Va.: McClure Printing, 1983.

Smith, Elmer L. *Meet The Mennonites in Pennsylvania Dutchland.* Lebanon, Pa.: Applied Arts Publishers, 1961.

Smith, Elmer Lewis, John G. Stewart, and M. Ellsworth Kyger. *The Penn-sylvania Germans of the Shenandoah Valley.* Allentown, Pa.: Pennsylva-nia German Folklore Society, 1964.

Sorrells, Nancy. "The Early Farm Landscape of the Shenandoah Valley." *Virginia Explorer* 11 (fall 1995): 18–23.

Stewart, John. "Shanghaiing in the Valley of Virginia." *Madison College Studies and Research Bulletin* 24 (February 1966): 97–105.

Stewart, John, and Elmer L. Smith. "An Occult Remedy Manuscript from Pendleton County, West Virginia." *Madison College Studies and Re-search Bulletin* 22 (February 1964): 77–85.

Stine, Eugene S. *Pennsylvania German Dictionary.* Birdsboro, Pa: Pennsyl-vania German Society, 1996.

Strickler, Harry M. *A Short History of Page County, Virginia.* Richmond, Va.: n.p., 1952.

Suter, Scott Hamilton. "Appreciating the Tree." *Virginia Explorer* 11 (fall 1995): 12–13.

———. " 'The Importance of Making Progress': The Potteries of Emanuel Suter, 1851–1897." Ph.D. diss., George Washington University, 1994.

———. *Tradition and Fashion: Cabinetmaking in the Upper Shenandoah Val-ley, 1850–1900.* Dayton, Va.: Shenandoah Valley Folk Art and Heritage Center, 1996.

————. "White Oak Basketmaking's Uncertain Future." *Upstream Magazine* 1 (September–October 1990): 6–7, 26.

Svenson, Peter. *Battlefield: Farming a Civil War Battleground.* Boston: Faber and Faber, 1992.

Terrell, I. L. *Old Houses in Rockingham County, 1750 to 1850.* Verona, Va.: McClure Press, 1970.

Thompson, Stith. *Motif-Index of Folk-Literature.* Bloomington: Indiana University Press, 1955–58.

Titon, Jeff Todd. *Powerhouse for God: Speech, Chant, and Song in an Appalachian Baptist Church.* Austin: University of Texas Press, 1988.

Toliver, Ruth M., ed. *History of Kelley Street United Brethren in Christ Church, Newtown, Harrisonburg, Virginia, 1892–1906.* N.p.: privately published, 1998.

Trout, W. E., III. *The Shenandoah River Atlas: Rediscovering the History of the Shenandoah and Its Branches.* Lexington, Va.: Virginia Canals and Navigations Society, 1997.

Tucker, George. *The Valley of Shenandoah; or, Memoirs of the Graysons.* 1824. Reprint, Chapel Hill: University of North Carolina Press, 1970.

Upton, Dell, ed. *America's Architectural Roots: Ethnic Groups That Built America.* Washington, D.C.: Preservation Press, 1986.

————. "Arts of the Virginia Germans." *Notes on Virginia* 19 (summer 1979): 3–7.

Virginia Traditions: Ballads from British Tradition. BRI-002. Ferrum, Va.: Blue Ridge Institute, n.d. Recording.

Vlach, John Michael. "The Concept of Community and Folklife Study." In *American Material Culture and Folklife: A Prologue and Dialogue,* ed. Simon J. Bronner, 63–75. Logan: Utah State University Press, 1992.

Waddell, Joseph A. *Annals of Augusta County, Virginia: From 1726–1871.* 2d ed. 1902. Reprint, Harrisonburg, Va.: C. J. Carrier, 1979.

Wayland, John W. *The German Element of the Shenandoah Valley of Virginia.* 1907. Reprint, Harrisonburg, Va.: C. J. Carrier, 1989.

————. *A History of Rockingham County, Virginia.* 1912. Reprint, Harrisonburg, Va.: C. J. Carrier, 1980.

————. *A History of Shenandoah County, Virginia.* Strasburg, Va.: Shenandoah Publishing House, 1927.

————. *Twenty-Five Chapters on the Shenandoah Valley.* 1957. Reprint, Harrisonburg, Va.: C. J. Carrier, 1976.

Weiser, Frederick S., and Howell J. Heany, eds. *The Pennsylvania German Fraktur of the Free Library of Philadelphia: An Illustrated Catalogue.* 2 vols. Breinigsville, Pa.: Pennsylvania German Society, 1976.

Wilson, Charles Reagan, and William Ferris, eds. *Encyclopedia of Southern Culture.* Chapel Hill: University of North Carolina Press, 1989.

Wiltshire, William E., III. *Folk Pottery of the Shenandoah Valley.* Intro. H. E. Comstock. New York: E. P. Dutton, 1975.

Wine, Joseph Floyd. *Life along Holman's Creek, Shenandoah County, Virginia.* Stephens City, Va.: Commercial Press, 1985.

———. *Tales from Shenandoah.* Stephens City, Va.: Commercial Press, 1989.

Wust, Klaus. *Folk Art in Stone: Southwest Virginia.* Edinburg, Va.: Shenandoah History, 1970.

———. "Fraktur and the Virginia Germans." *Arts in Virginia* 14 (fall 1974): 2–3.

———. *Virginia Fraktur: Penmanship as Folk Art.* Edinburg, Va.: Shenandoah History, 1972.

———. *The Virginia Germans.* Charlottesville: University Press of Virginia, 1969.

Yoder, Don. "Folk Medicine." In *Folklore and Folklife: An Introduction,* ed. Richard Dorson, 191–215. Chicago: University of Chicago Press, 1972.

———. "Fraktur in Mennonite Culture." *Mennonite Quarterly Review* 48 (1974): 305–42.

———. "Official Religion versus Folk Religion." *Pennsylvania Folklife* 15 (1965–66): 36–52.

———. "Toward a Definition of Folk Religion." *Western Folklore* 33 (1974): 2–15.

Zarrugh, Laura. "Report of Subcommittee on Immigrant Groups." Harrisonburg, Va.: Refugee Resettlement Office, 1997.